i Forgive
An Inner Lane Toward Forgiveness

Kevin Beneby

i Forgive
An Inner Lane Toward Forgiveness

© Copyright 2020 Kevin Beneby

Published by
21st Century Press
Springfield, MO 65807

21st Century Press is a Christian publisher dedicated to publishing books that have a high standard of family values. We believe the vision for our company is to provide families and individuals with user-friendly materials that will help them in their daily lives and experiences. It is our prayer that this book will help you discover biblical truth for your own life and help you meet the needs of others. May God richly bless you.

Scripture taken from the NEW AMERICAN STANDARD BIBLE, Copyright 1960, 1962, 1963, 1968, 1971, 1972, 1973, 1975, 1995 by The Lockman Foundation. Used by permission.

The Holy Bible: New Revised Standard Version. 1989. Nashville: Thomas Nelson Publishers.

21st Century Press
2131 W. Republic Rd, MB 211
Springfield MO 65807
email: lee@21stcenturypress.com

Cover Design: Lee Fredrickson
Book Design: Lee Fredrickson

ISBN: TBook: 978-1-951774-15-8
      Ebook: 978-1-951774-22-6

Visit our website at: www.21stcenturypress.com
Printed in the United States of America

21stCENTURY
P   R   E   S   S
READING YOU LOUD AND CLEAR

Dedication

To Denise, whose vision, support, and encouragement helped to make this project a reality! To Kenan, Abishai, and Denereus whose understanding spirits have created the context for their endurance of the necessary sacrifices!

Acknowledgments

Profound appreciation and acknowledgment is extended to my immediate and church families! To my mother, sister and brothers, the members of Highbury Park church of Christ, West Side church of Christ in Searcy AR, and the Hutchinson Mountain church of Christ who have helped to shape the contours of my personhood in their own unique ways.

For me, acknowledgments will be incomplete if there is no mention of the instructors at Harding University; particularly, those attached to the Bible Department and the Center for Advanced Ministry Training, whose robust and comprehensive approach to ministry training has exposed and expanded me.

Special appreciation is extended to the instructors in my Marriage and Family Therapy training. Along with my cohort members, they have caused me to be awakened to the psychological dimensions of my human experience. Through them I have a fuller appreciation of self and others.

My Creator must be acknowledged as well, for He has given me the strength and the capacity to bring together the relevant parts of this undertaking.

Contents

Foreword

Sooner or later every one of us will either offend another or be offended, or both. It is inevitable and will, most likely, happen many times. Often, we don't know how to forgive or to be forgiven. For us to be able and willing to forgive when we have been mistreated or abused is very important. Our heavenly Father instructed us to be ready to forgive one who sins against us. In Matthew 6:14-15, Jesus said, "For if ye forgive men their trespasses your heavenly Father will also forgive you. But, if you forgive not men their trespasses neither will your Father forgive your trespasses."

If we want God to forgive us when we sin against Him, we must truly and willingly forgive others. Kevin Beneby, in his book, *I Forgive: An Inner Lane Toward Forgiveness*, has included biblical injunctions as well as practical reasoning, suggestions, and solutions to help us react appropriately to any offense. His examples and suggestions will be helpful to the reader as the need for forgiveness occurs. Thanks to the author for his biblical and practical treatment of a subject that affects us all.

I have known Kevin Beneby for several years and appreciate his love for the Lord, His Word, and His creation. Reading his book and following his suggestions will help anyone to be more faithful to God and more faithful to family, friends, and associates..

Dr. Clifton Ganus,
Former President of Harding University

I Forgive

Introduction

L ife is full of disappointments, disillusionments, and offenses. In 1939 the war machinery of Adolf Hitler's Nazi-led Germany began to advance its assault against neighboring countries. The pretext for such actions was partly due to Germany's lack of contentment with the Treaty of Versailles it was forced to enter at the end of World War I. The agreement resulted in the reduction of Germany's territory.

Additionally, the machinery was motivated by an ideology of racial supremacy that spawned hatred towards Jews resulting in the systematic extermination of some six million of them through executions, starvation, and gassing, followed by mass cremations at concentration camps. The progressive change in the approach used to kill the Jews was driven by a need to find a quicker and more efficient way to exterminate high numbers that were being killed.

At the end of World War II, Hitler's regime would be considered a major catalyst for and contributor to the destruction of some sixty million people.

Another notable chapter in man's history chronicles the many cases of abuse that were birthed out of the slave trade where one race, again, imposed its ideology of racial supremacy over another. Because of it, many Negroes were "raked" from their homes in Africa, resulting in families being torn apart and subjected to unimaginable cruelty that has only seen the end stage of significant mitigation as late as the 1960's. Such cruelty still has a residual impact on race relations today in the United States of America.

On September 11th, 2001, the United States of America became the object of an elaborate plan of al-Qaeda operatives led by one Osama Bin Laden. The world was in shock as members of this group seized possession of commercial jetliners and commandeered them, hitting prominent US targets, including the Twin Towers of the World Trade Center that were situated in New York. At the end of that fateful day, over three thousand people lost their lives.

Several employees of the automaker, Volkswagen, deliberately manipulated their vehicles' computer software so that they would create false readings regarding emission specifications. Another automaker, General Motors Company, ignored faulty ignition switches in their vehicles, leading to the deaths of some twelve persons.

The halls of academia have seen their share of injury perpetrated by students and teachers alike. One account reveals a university lecturer who did not clarify his expectations for students' class participation at the beginning of a course. However, he still held students accountable for it at the end of the semester.

A pastor, having been entrusted with the task of counseling a challenged teenage female, found himself in a compromised position as he abused the trust reposed in him by family members when he engaged in a protracted sexual relationship with the young lady.

Principled in nature, another young lady, a virgin, deviated from her cultural mores of sexual relationships before marriage because she wanted to keep herself sexually whole for her husband. However, she was drugged and raped by someone she trusted. She was left violated, and in such a state of depression that she experienced suicidal ideation.

A group of men entered a residence that was home to a school-teacher and her hard-working husband. The motive appeared to be robbery because a truck was taken from the residence. However, that was not all that was taken. The aftermath of the robbery scene revealed the brutal execution-style murders of the couple, the news of which rocked a local community.

In the beautiful archipelago country of the Bahamas, a mentally deranged man, with homosexual tendencies, systematically lured young boys into his web of deceit. He killed them and buried their bodies only to revisit their graves and further desecrate their remains.

Having been recently promoted, a young man is coping nicely with his new environment and co-workers. As far as he is concerned, things are going well. However, one day, he learns the true nature of his work environment. A friendly "whistleblower," one of his co-workers, calls him over to her desk and informs him, in animated fashion, that some of his co-workers wanted him to fail. Apparently, some still had a "soft spot" for the young man's predecessor.

A father abandons his home. He abdicates his responsibility towards his wife and children because of another woman, forgetting the pledge he made to his wife when they entered the covenant of marriage and the nurturing role that he functioned in as a father.

In another instance, and despite the absence of a doubt, from a physical or biological perspective (for the son looks like him), a father categorically denies that his son belongs to him. Consequently, the son grew up without the acknowledgment, affirmation, nurturing, love, and modeling of a father.

In a junior high school, the cordial relationship of two close female schoolmates was dismantled when a major dispute erupted over a pencil.

Two friends had a good relationship. One would store his lunch in the cupboard of the other; this was the pattern for a long time. One day there was a bitter argument between them, to the bewilderment of observers. The reason for the dispute was a mystery, even to one of the parties involved. The following day, when asked why he and his friend argued so bitterly after they had enjoyed such an amicable relationship, he responded, "I went home and asked myself the same thing!"

With a cool and easygoing walk towards his truck, an employee is about to make a bank deposit for the company he works for. However, as he enters his vehicle, a "gun-wheeling" robber suddenly appears on the scene, with expert timing. The employee is accosted. Startled and with an aggressive maneuver, the employee tries to close the door of his truck to ward off the attack, but the robber pulls the door open with greater force. He then fatally shoots the employee, climbs into the truck, and picks up the deposit bag, making good his escape in a waiting vehicle that sped off into the flow of traffic.

It was a cool afternoon, and a motorist was enjoying a nice leisurely drive in her convertible, with its top down. However, such an experience was problematic for another driver who, in passing the leisure driver, honked his horn out of displeasure over how slow she was driving. The story does not end there! The leisure driver seemed to have moved quickly from a tranquil mood into one of aggression and anger, for she hotly pursued the driver of the honking vehicle and gave him "a piece of her mind."

There was another motorist who was very conscientious of the speed limit while driving in one of the left lanes of a four-lane dual carriageway. However, a truck from the rear starts to overtake his vehicle, and just as the driver of the truck made eye contact with him, he flipped him the "birdie," leaving him to try and figure out what he did wrong.

A taxi driver described how a woman ran into the front of his car with her vehicle, causing significant damage. After the collision, she came out of her vehicle and told the taxi driver that she would fix his vehicle. However, the taxi driver did not want to go that route. He wanted the accident to be investigated properly by a police officer that was near the accident dealing with another matter. The taxi driver advised the woman to pull her vehicle to the side of the road (which he was also prepared to do), in order to wait for the officer. She sped off in her vehicle, leaving the scene of the accident.

A wife finds evidence that exposed a secret sexual relationship of her husband. The revelation, of which, placed their marriage on "rocky grounds."

Another husband showed disregard for his wife and their marital vows as he, in a systematic fashion, engaged in multiple affairs, spanning many years. Injury to his wife was further exacerbated, as he would use their sacred bedroom chambers to carry out some of his treacherous sexual exploits.

Here is a case that is more personal to me! My father, a grocer, who had just celebrated his 93rd birthday, was badly beaten with a hammer and crowbar and left to die in his store. The pair of criminals who perpetrated the crime successfully eluded justice, even as I currently type these words. However, the violent incident carried out against an elderly person provides a good example of the terrible moral decay that can reside in the human character and society.

INTRODUCTION

As seen in the above vignettes, offenses come in many shapes and sizes. Some cut more deeply than others, and from your experiences, you probably know that some are handled or navigated more easily than others. I am cognizant that some offenses cause so much pain that to immediately broach the idea of forgiving an offender may not be appropriate due to the gravity and impact of the offense; indeed, to have regard for such a position, in an offense, is reasonable.

However, beyond the immediacy of the offensive situation and against the background of: "Forgiveness is divine, I am only human"; "I can't forgive him"; "I can't forgive her"; "It is too difficult to forgive"; "God is in the forgiving business, I am not"; and, "I will never forgive…for what was done to me." And as an option in dealing with an offense, I want to pose a question for our consideration: As we consider offenses perpetrated against our person, can such offenses be forgiven?

As we will see, forgiving an offender does not necessarily mean that the variables of justice and other consequences connected to an offense are withstood. Yet still, as an option, I want to put the above question on the "table" of your mind.

The request of the Nigerians, when they would offend, comes to mind: "Please, can you find a place in your heart to forgive me?" Is this an idle request, or is it an appeal that suggests the capacity of the one being entreated to forgive?

You may be reading this book because you want to forgive an offender, but you are finding it extremely difficult to do so. Or, there may be difficulty in forgiving yourself. Perhaps, you want to shore up your experiences with extending forgiveness. It may be that you wish to become more acquainted with the subject of forgiveness by acquiring the knowledge of how you can extend forgiveness, when the need arises.

Still, you just may be exploring the subject of forgiveness because you have a friend who is struggling with it, and you want to help them. There also might be a particular subtopic in the table of contents that has captured your attention. Whatever the reason, you will find a wealth of information on this timely and relevant topic.

Let me encourage you to read the work in its entirety because the topic is presented from a systematic perspective (the information in

15

the various chapters are connected). As you continue to read, you will be exposed to a concept of extending forgiveness that factors in theological underpinnings while paying respect to our psychological and biological makeup. Regarding the biblical quotes, my brief explanation of the citations will be in parenthesis!

The inspired quotes of Karen Woodside (a pseudonym) will preface some of the information that is revealed in this work. They will help with the tenor of the subject matter. When Woodside came to the clinical setting, she was greatly distressed and filled with self-blame over her husband's incestuous relationship with their daughter. She also recognized that if she wanted to obtain the Creator's forgiveness, it was hinged on her ability to forgive the one who had grievously offended her. She acknowledged this but still wanted to exact vengeance. She wanted to inflict injury on her husband, the one who had violated their daughter.

This strong yearning to carry out a payback was also fueled by the surreptitious stance of her husband – according to Woodside, he had carried out his abuse on their daughter "right under my nose." Her anger was deepened by the fact that she, in her naivety and goodwill, felt that she had been taken advantage of. Such anger was understandable!

Nevertheless, she acknowledged her tension: seeking the Creator's forgiveness in her life was predicated on her forgiving the "monster of a person" whose head she felt like smashing in. She needed help in entering the region of extending forgiveness, as well as navigating the tumultuous time in her life.

I have two confessions to make. First, I am not an avid professional athlete. Except for my "flexible" three times a week thirty-minute aerobic exercise regiment, I am far removed from the arenas of track and field and other sporting activities in general.

However, I remember, in my experience with such arenas, there might be an advantage for the athlete competing in the inner lane. So, a potential advantage exists for the athlete in the inner lane, even if it is only found in a psychological and/or subjective view and perception that one has the advantage in the inner lane.

At the start of a race, the athlete closest to, or in the inner lane, can have the advantage for they hear the sound of the starting gun before the others do, as that sound takes longer to reach those in the outer lanes. Notwithstanding the efforts of sports officials to mitigate such an advantage, I want to acknowledge here that such an advantage can exist.

Therefore, the advantage of the inner lane serves as a fitting figure for what I am attempting to do, and that is to offer you an advantage so you would consider forgiving an offender or be helped in the process, notwithstanding how difficult it may be.

Second, I must confess that as I studied for and worked with this undertaking, at times, I felt a sense of inadequacy in addressing such a sensitive issue. Feelings of inadequacy existed because extending forgiveness to offenders can be so challenging for us as human beings; indeed, it can be quite formidable.

Additionally, our individual personas make it such that going through the process of extending forgiveness is unique to each person. Therefore, there is no "cookie-cutter" mold that all of us can fit into.

Still, I am encouraged in the view that I may have something to offer that can help you on your path to, or in your struggle with, forgiving an offender. Are you ready? Buckle up! Let's go to the frontier of extending forgiveness.

I Forgive

Chapter One

The Context of Offenses

Our introduction provides us with a minuscule sample of offenses. What is implied from that sample is we live in a world or context of offenses. A cycle of offending has gripped humanity! Sometimes we are offended, and sometimes we offend.

Jesus, the Christ, and spiritual leader of Christians put it profoundly: "Woe to the world because of its stumbling blocks [*offenses*]! For it is inevitable that stumbling blocks come; but woe to that man through whom the stumbling block comes" (Matthew 18:7).

The profundity of Jesus' statement presents a truth about the human experience: There will be behaviors that produce hindrances and hurdles in the interpersonal experiences between man and man, as well as between man and his Creator. Yet, I want to point out quickly that not all our human experiences are characterized as being offensive. There are behaviors that can be described as good or noble, as man functions in his sojourn on earth.

For instance, on September 1st, 2019, hurricane Dorian began to devastate two of the northern islands of the Bahamas, specifically, Abaco and Grand Bahama. Many homes were destroyed during the passing of the hurricane, and parts of those islands were deemed uninhabitable. In a spirit of care and concern, many countries and organizations swiftly came to the aid of the people of the Bahamas with monetary and human resources. There were even cruise companies that redirected their ships to aid in the evacuation of people on the impacted islands.

Such concern and aid, offered by human beings, was commendable and underscores the fact that people can act beneficently towards one another. And so, we have the co-existence of the good and the bad (offenses), as we consider man's behavior.

19

Specifics Regarding the Context of Offenses

Seeing that we are focusing on the context within which offenses occur, which is an important consideration when looking at the concept of extending forgiveness or forgiving an offender, it is necessary that we reflect further on what an offense is and the variables that contribute to it. As indicated above, implied within the term, offenses are hindrances and hurdles that interfere with the health of our interpersonal relations and man's relationship with his Creator.

However, at the root of an offense is a breach of some moral understanding or law; some code is violated. Due to the violation, the offended is left diminished or devalued in some way. Therefore, accompanying an offense is a debt that the offender owes the offended.

The Nature of Offenses

An *offense may be unique to a relationship*. A wife may be offended or upset that her husband was derelict in his duties and allowed her cookies to be burnt in the oven. Indeed, what may be an offense in one relationship may not be in another. *Offenses can occur between neighbors.* When one borrows a neighbor's lawnmower and does not return it in a timely fashion, this may offend the neighbor – borrowing the lawnmower the next time may not be as easy. *Offenses may occur between nations.* When Japan, purposefully and without provocation, attacked the United States of America's Pearl Harbor Naval Base, resulting in the loss of many lives, an offense took place.

Today, if individuals were to consider the code for living, as laid down in the Bible, for followers of Christ and, indeed, for human beings everywhere, they would conclude that *many of us offend the Creator* when we break His code. For instance, Christians are forbidden to steal: "He who steals must steal no longer; but rather he must labor, performing with his own hands what is good, so that he will have something to share with one who has need" (Ephesians 4:28). Consequently, if a Christian steals, they have offended their Creator.

Another important point to consider is the fact that *intentionality*, good or bad, may characterize an offense. An individual may deliberately skim monies from the boss' cash register only to be caught on camera. Even though the intentions might have been to repay the money after a while, an offense occurred.

However, some offenses may be *unintentional*. Unaware of her husband's mortified and uncomfortable feelings, a wife begins to talk about bedroom matters at the dinner table with another couple. The husband patiently waits to address the issue alone with his wife (a noble approach, indeed). After such an unintentional offense, the husband moves deliberately to inform his wife of how he felt having been offended, and together they set a different course for future conversations with others.

As we have described above, there is a cross-section of circumstances that can lead to offenses, but it must be borne in mind that not all offenses are of equal weight. To offend an individual by burning the cookies does not carry the same weight as offending the Creator when one steals from someone. In other words, burning the cookies, in and of itself, is not offensive (a sin) before our Creator; however, stealing, which goes against His design for the human experience, is an offense.

Why Are We offended?

Although it may not seem like it at times, there are *moral standards* that govern us as human beings. While in specific cultures, such standards may vary, I believe that they are from our Creator, and it is He that brings greater definition to them through His word found in the Bible. I also believe that if we search the nations, for the most part, we will find that it is horribly offensive for a forty-five-year-old man to violate a six-year-old girl sexually. Also, we will discover that among the nations, there is something detestable about breaking into someone's home and plundering their belongings. Additionally, the intentional murder of someone is not accepted or sanctioned in the nations.

Even as an individual may repudiate the code of God presented in the Bible, yet as they would function in society, in the work environment, on the streets of a city, or at dinner in a restaurant, they do so with a sense of "oughtness" or moral obligation.

With this concept in mind, we can appreciate why we are offended. Take the case of a sick, bedridden wife! The husband, as well as the wife, feels that it is his duty to ensure that she has something to eat. If he does not feed her or make certain that she is fed, an offense occurs. Why? Because such offense comes out of a sense of perceived obligation, as well as expectation, that dictates he takes care of her in this way. When he does not respond accordingly or in harmony with the wife's expectations, she is offended. When we do not act appropriately or the way we ought to, we offend one another.

Furthermore, humans are social beings! While it is critical for us to have individual identity, functionality, and resources in relationships, we also seek for intimacy, association, and connectedness with one another. Through these, we build our families, neighborhoods, and societies in a spirit of togetherness and cooperation. The protagonist, played by actor Tom Hanks, in the movie, *Cast Away*, illustrates our quest for connectedness.

Hanks found himself on an isolated island after a plane crash. Eventually, he is able to find sustenance – he starts fires, eats coconuts, and catches fish. He even begins a relationship with a personified volleyball that he called, "Wilson," after its brand name. Yet, he was not content to remain on the isolated island despite his accomplishments. For him, something was desired or missing in isolation.

So, he made a raft and sought to cross a dangerous water barrier that surrounded the island. After trying to cross the barrier more than once, and incurring injury in doing so, his persistence paid off, and he escaped the trap and isolation of the island, that is, he and "Wilson." Why the desire to leave the island even though it sustained him? In the movie, the delivery of a package seemed to be the motivation, but it is conceivable that Hanks' departure from the island became a goal out of his desire for human connectedness.

I once heard a story told of a prison inmate who was placed in solitary confinement because of some breach in prison policy. After the inmate was released from confinement and placed back into the general prison population, it was observed that he met up with a fellow prisoner and began to talk incessantly to him. The fellow prisoner found it difficult to get a word in; it seemed as though the inmate had missed being around people and needed to connect with someone.

These accounts illustrate just how much we are created for to-getherness, that is, we need to connect with fellow humans, and for good reasons too – for the company, procreation, friendship, support, encouragement, and accomplishments, to name a few. However, our desire to be with others also positions us for the possibility of being offended by those we seek to connect with.

This brings me to my next point regarding why we are susceptible to being offended. Whether it is an endeavor to strengthen the ties in fam-ily relationships, seeking greater intimacy with a beloved spouse, or en-tering into a business partnership, there is something that is concurrent with the desire to build in such relations - *risk*. Because we are willing to take *risks for relational gain*, we find ourselves vulnerable to offenses.

I do not want to portray a view that something is wrong with risk-taking, for it is one of the pathways to success. Indeed, if we had greater amounts of people taking more risks, who knows where these individuals, their families, or even their societies would be? But risk and vulnerability are like two peas in a pod – experiencing one means that we are also experiencing the other.

A word about intimacy – it is important to note that our Creator has forged an intimate relationship with every human being before intimacy is realized between a mother and her unborn infant growing in her womb, or the intimacy sought and found in a spouse. Hear the psalmist, as he refers to the Creator in a biblical text:

> For You formed my inward parts; You wove me in my mother's womb. I will give thanks to You, for I am fearfully and wonderfully made; wonderful are Your works, and my soul knows it very well. My frame was not hidden from You, when I was made in secret, and skillfully wrought in the depths of the earth. Your eyes have seen my unformed substance; and in Your book were all written the days that were ordained for me, when as yet there was not one of them (Psalm 139:13-16).

Another biblical text puts it this way: "Thus declares the Lord who stretches out the heavens, lay the foundation of the earth, and forms the spirit of man within him" (Zachariah 12:1).

It is very apparent that the Creator is intimate with each one of us, and more so than any human intimacy realized. Just think about it! From our gestation period in the womb, which is characterized by the development of critical body systems, to provisions in our lives outside the womb that are essential to our survival on earth, they all reflect someone, that is, our Creator, who is deeply intimate with us. It amazes me that right out of the womb; babies have all that they need to get started with their development – they have the ability to cry, as well as they display grasping and sucking behaviors, just to name a few.

Who has caused there to be an interlocking of the alveoli in our lungs and the air surrounding us, which facilitates the critical absorption and release of bodily gases? Who has caused there to be an interlocking of our stomachs and food from the ground, and where we can say that each has been prepared for the other? Look at your hands. Think for a moment about moving them, and then move them. If you did that "simple" exercise, know that it was made possible by your Creator and not some random act of chance.

Our thought processes are underpinned by our brain's biological functioning, and they together constitute our mind, which is the handiwork of the One who is deeply acquainted with us. The eyes, with their special muscles, ligaments, and tendons that allow us to focus on everything in our field of vision, even the very eyes that you are using to read this book, bear the marks of a Designer who knows what it takes for us to function on earth.

What I want to convey here is that we take risks as we seek intimacy and connectedness with our fellow human beings, but we are not the only ones in the business of risk-taking. Our existence reveals that the Creator has also taken a great risk in forging an incomprehensible level of intimacy with us. He, too, can be offended as He seeks to build on such intimacy with us humans.

Why Do We Offend?

Johnny, a newlywed, physically abuses his wife when she disagrees with him about how their monies should be spent. This response is not an isolated one, for there is an emerging pattern of hitting his wife when there is a disagreement. While there is no excuse for Johnny's propensity to beat his wife, it can be asked, "Why does Johnny respond to disagreements with his wife the way he does, instead of talking it through?" There is a statement in the world of psychology that goes like this: "The pattern one knows is the pattern one knows." This statement helps us to provide a possible context for Johnny's tendency to hit his wife. The act of hitting might have stemmed from the modeled behavior that he saw in his father in his family of origin.

Johnny saw his father hit his mother whenever she disagreed with him. Because this pattern was placed before Johnny during his formative years and now that he has taken on a wife, he engages in it. Johnny's act of hitting his wife is offensive, but the behavior or practice can be traced to learned patterns in his family of origin.

As indicated earlier, sometimes, when an offense occurs, it was not the offender's intention to offend. In fact, offending someone may not have even been in our conscious minds. The offense may stem from unconscious defensive mechanisms that have their origins in impaired or unhealthy emotional attachments with our caregiver(s) when we were babies, young, and developing. There is a whole science around such a view that is delineated in what is known as the attachment theory[1] in the world of psychotherapy.

The theory holds that emotional attachments can be secure between caregiver and caretaker. A secure attachment is characterized by a mutual emotional coordination, disruption, and repair. This can be illustrated in a toddler that is used to seeing the encouraging smiling face of his father and interprets such a face as permission to carry on his exploring, as toddlers normally do. However, during one of his exploits, the toddler pulls on the dining room's tablecloth and causes some of the set dinnerware to fall off the table onto the floor and break.

The father approaches the toddler with an upset face and verbally rebukes him. The toddler begins to cry. Here, there is a disruption in the emotional coordination between father and toddler. The father then picks up the crying toddler and smiles at him, giving him the assurance that he is still present as encourager and caregiver. The toddler stops crying. The emotional disruption was repaired. The tablecloth incident will act as an adaptive experience for the toddler. He then carries on with his exploits, hopefully not pulling on the tablecloth because of the lesson learned.

Secure attachments offer developing individuals the resources they need to effectively navigate the emotional interpersonal engagements to the extent that, in adulthood, they become attuned to theirs' and others' emotional depositions. Consequently, they can feel and deal emotionally with others, be it a spouse, boss, friend, neighbor, or even themselves. We can tell then that secure emotional attachments go a long way in fostering healthy relationships.

What happens when secure emotional attachments are absent in individuals? This gives rise to what is called insecure attachments. These are also characterized by mutual emotional coordination between caregiver and caretaker. However, when a disruption occurs, there is failure in the caregiver to repair the relationship. Resulting, as traumatic episodes are encountered, in the developing caretaker entering a state of survival and protection of themselves by unconsciously and/or consciously employing coping and defensive mechanisms – beneath which, are the core/inner emotions of fear and/or shame. Therefore, the mutual emotional coordination between caregiver and caretaker is interrupted, in their secure attachments, and if not repaired, emotional coordination becomes impaired.

Consequently, the individual with insecure emotional attachments may deal and not feel emotionally with individuals in an avoidant pattern. Or they might feel and not deal emotionally in an ambivalent pattern. Defensive mechanisms contribute to the avoidance and ambivalence and are in the way of healthy emotional relationships.

Even in such cases, we must note that the unconscious "blueprints" for individuals' emotional engagements are laid down during their developmental stages through emotional coordination in caregiver/caretaker relationships. And while defensive mechanisms can serve a vital survival purpose, particularly, in the cases of severe traumatic experiences, they often find themselves out of context in the here and now, resulting in unhealthy interpersonal relationships. This helps to explain why we may sometimes offend in our unconscious defensiveness and not realize it.

For instance, a wife may have a problem with an emotionally inse-cure attached husband who does not respond with the warm embrace or hug that she expects when she feels and expresses the frustrations of her day. Therefore, he offends his wife because he does not engage her emotionally. Actually, it is possible that the hug is not forthcoming because the husband, in his family of origin, might have become emo-tionally desensitized through a defensive mechanism in an avoidance pattern that prevents him from feeling and responding appropriately to his wife.

A bit more needs to be said about the offensive traumatic episodes we encounter during and after our early developmental stages. Trauma can be viewed as a negative experience that continues to affect our person and functionality, negatively.[2] In the field of psychology, minor traumatic experiences are referred to as *small–T traumas,*" and major experiences are designated *"large–T traumas."*[3]

Large or small, trauma can invoke our bodies' survival responses: to the point where, because certain vehement feelings and emotions are so painful, they are dissociated/disconnected or repressed in our brain functions. Such feelings and emotions can become fragmented, unpro-cessed, non-integrated, "undigested," and in a term I prefer, "non-con-textualized." They find themselves out of the conscious narratives of in-dividuals experiencing them, yet they exert their negative effects; those suffering from the anxiety disorder of Post-Traumatic Stress Disorder (PTSD), is an example of this.

Traumatic experiences impact us differently due to several reasons. Secure emotional attachments or the lack thereof can determine the impact of trauma on our person. Support structures in our environ-ment can also determine how we process trauma.

The overwhelming nature of the traumatic experience itself can have such a physiological impact that brain biology, and bodily func-tions are altered. This is easily appreciated, in the case of the violent offensive rape of a woman who continually has intrusive mental flash-backs, possibly triggered by a scent or items in a similar context as that of the violation, even years after the traumatic experience.

Fortunately, such emotional disconnects and feelings, along with their problematic defenses, in insecure attachments and traumatic experiences, can be repaired or healed through the process of psychotherapy. The alliance with a therapist can go a long way in helping individuals to "contextualize" "non-contextualized" feelings and attain emotional healing. The therapeutic alliance promotes such healing because, in a safe context, therapists affirm, support, and challenge their clients while empathizing with them.

Therapists' use of psychological therapeutic models such as Accelerated Experiential Dynamic Psychotherapy (AEDP)[4] and Eye Movement Desensitization and Reprocessing (EMDR)[5] can help individuals address impaired emotional attachments and traumatic experiences. These approaches aid in the lowering of problematic defenses (and offenses they may lead to), apprehension of unconscious feelings, and effective management of core (inner) emotions, all of which are critical for the health of interpersonal relations and individual functionality. If you, as a reader, realize that you can benefit from an alliance with a therapist, then let me encourage you to seek one out that is apt to help you.

Character Flaws

As we consider further the factors that lead individuals to offend others, selfishness should not be left out of the picture. I am speaking about that aspect of the human character that looks out for its own interests, regardless of the cost to others. In it, the interests of others are not tabulated. Out of this selfishness, people also offend when they commit murder or adultery, as well as a whole host of other vices.

What is being discussed here must not be confused with a balanced perspective and embrace of one's selfhood, which is comprised of self-awareness, self-confidence, self-achievement, self-esteem, self-renewal, and the necessary "me-time." What is being delineated in this offensive selfishness is seen through the violent killing of a businessman, with dependents, over a mobile phone. The perpetrator of such a callous act destroyed a valuable life just to satisfy his materialistic craving. This offensive selfishness then can be understood as an act perpetrated by someone who sought to satisfy his appetite while ignoring the personhood, wellbeing, and feelings of others.

Intolerance, in its many shapes and forms, is another contributor that leads some individuals to offend others. Racial intolerance continues to pervade the landscape of many countries. It often gives birth to offenses through verbal assaults and bias in ethnic dealings. And it incubates the devaluation of fellow human beings. The brutal massacres that occurred between the Tutsi and Hutu tribes of Rwanda have left a stain on the human experience. They showcase what can happen when intolerance finds good soil and is allowed to germinate and mature.

While intolerance and the offenses that it spawns can be seen through racial tensions, the same is experienced "intra-racially" or within a race. Before I progress, I would like to add that the need to tolerate one another does not necessarily mean that we have to agree with what is being said or adhere to what is being done in the various subgroups of society. Neither does it mean that there is not a standard outside our differences that ought to govern us. This tolerance directs us to be respectful towards each other, as we help one another navigate the issues of life.

Notwithstanding the above considerations, intolerance within any particular race can abound; especially, when it comes to religion and political matters. And where intolerance goes, offense is sure to follow!

Also, our immediate relationships provide the opportunity for intolerance. The co-worker that seems to be a bit eccentric at times may prove to be a challenge to tolerate, especially when the boss puts both of you to work on an assignment together. Do you see the many opportunities for offense-creation in this coupling? Do you see the potential for stonewalling, contempt, and disdain?

Marriage is an example of another immediate relationship where we can find this offensive intolerance. While a lifetime of togetherness with a beloved spouse can be very enriching, when intolerance is permitted to fester, the institution can be personally exhausting. Offense is inevitable when a husband has the tendency to truncate conversations with his wife stating, "Okay, I don't want to talk about it anymore. I have had enough!" This is especially the case if the wife is engaging but is sometimes long-winded. Offense comes when she hears her husband's words that interrupt her verbal profusion pouring out of *the self*.

As you reflect on the above scenario, what do you think is a possible antidote for the husband and wife's dilemma? From a systematic point of view, there may be some issues that the husband might need to address that brought him to the point of intolerance. But if your answer prescribes that the husband should increase his tolerance of his wife's communication style, as she would tolerate his, then I would agree with you. At least it will be the starting point for the husband to maintain unfettered intimate access to his wife's core (inner) self without her becoming anxious or defensive and wondering if their conversation has reached some ambiguous cap off point.

Since intolerance feeds offenses, it can be viewed as an act stemming from a prideful, haughty disposition. When these are a part of a person's character, humility is noticeably absent. Humility allows us to engage each other respectfully! It allows us to view the other person through an understanding of our own existence.

So, as much as I would appreciate my creaturely nature and all the rights and privileges that come along with it, and the fact that I would not want them to be taken away from me, I would want the same for my fellow human beings, in the spirit of humility.

It takes humility, that lowly mindset, to ensure that the rights and privileges of another, bestowed upon them by the Creator, are respected. You know those rights and privileges: the right to be seen, the right to be heard, the privilege to impact others with one's giftedness; and, the privilege of making a difference in our world, to name a few.

The Broader Perspective of an Offense

In discussing the three contributors to offenses (selfishness, intolerance, and a haughty attitude) above, our humanistic character flaws have been manifested. Through them, we can realize that there is an influence outside of ourselves. Certain offensive behaviors are not in harmony with the Creator's design for the human experience. This is partly evident by what Scripture reveals: "He has told you, O man, what is good; And what does the Lord require of you but to do justice, to love kindness, and to walk humbly with your God" (Micah 6:8)?

Do you see a bit of the ideal in the Creator's design for the human experience? It is an ideal that places human beings within a context that fosters togetherness, fairness, cooperation, support, goodwill, and unified achievements. This context is free from the offenses that find their maturation in the character flaws found in humans, like the ones mentioned above.

Therefore, we are or should be drawn to consider something (an influence) beyond ourselves, which is not a difficult proposition. After all, there are some things about our existence that reveal that we are more than flesh and blood. Yes, our composition is more than our physical makeup! The ability to think, for instance, comes to mind. We can reflect on our actions, before and after they occur, in the inner processes of our minds. And these mental processes have their abode in the invisible dimension of the human experience called the spirit or heart of man, which is the inner self or the actual self that dwells inside our bodies.

This spirit man, given by the Creator, animates the body. Why is there a stillness of the body when someone dies? Because the part of man that animates the body has departed. There is a part of man that makes us different from the animals, the spirit part, and this part can be influenced by our Creator or another being called Satan or the devil.

Like the Creator, who represents goodwill towards people and wants to influence us, Satan, who represents ill will towards humanity, also wants to influence us. Scripture, as it addresses those who now please their Creator, reveals that Satan has a stronghold on, or significant influence over, the lives of those who do not please Him:

> And you were dead in your trespasses and sins, in which you formerly walked according to the course of this world, according to the prince of the power of the air, of the spirit that is now working in the sons of disobedience. Among them we too all formerly lived in the lusts of our flesh, indulging the desires of the flesh and of the mind and were by nature children of wrath, even as the rest (Ephesians 2:1-3).

So, as we consider certain offenses, our perspective of their origin must be enlarged. Offenses perpetrated against fellow human beings that result in the breaking of the Creator's code for our earthly sojourn can be traced back to the influence of Satan, who is the Creator's, as well as humanity's enemy. Such offenses have a double impact, impeding a wholesome relationship with our fellow human beings and the Creator. If I commit adultery with my neighbor's wife, not only do I offend my neighbor, but I also offend my Creator. For His code regarding the institution of marriage requires that it be given respect by those in and outside of it.

While Satan influences certain offenses, yet this understanding does not absolve us of our role in and accountability for them. As humans, we are free to choose whose influence we would want to govern our lives, Satan, or the Creator's. I can then conclude that when it comes to breaking the Creator's code, Satan can only exert his influence in my life to the extent that I allow him to.

We looked, a bit, at what is going on within our context of offenses. Like bees, we are social creatures, having been enjoined to the Creator's code that ought to govern our interpersonal relationships.

We were created to connect with fellow human beings; we crave it and seek it. But this makes us vulnerable to human offenses, which have their root in the emotional deficits and traumatic experiences we have encountered in our formative years.

Such human offenses, while they are manifested through our character flaws, beyond ourselves, are also influenced by a spiritual being – the devil. Who, like the Creator, can also influence our spirit nature and thus our behavior! However, this understanding is not to absolve us of our responsibility and accountability in our decision-making. But it expands our view of the genesis of some offenses, particularly, those that violate the Creator's code for our lives. It is important now for us to look at the impact of offenses on our person.

For further deliberation...

1.   The stigma attached to going to a clinical psychotherapist is still alive in society. How might we mitigate against it?

2. What do you think is necessary to appreciate behaviors that do and do not offend the Creator?

3. How can we have a better appreciation of our mutual moral "ought-ness?"

4. Why should we have regard for intimacy with our fellow human beings and the Creator?

5. Do you believe that there is a spiritual dimension of our existence influenced by spiritual beings beyond us? Why or why not?

I Forgive

Chapter Two

It Hurts!

"I feel like going up to him and smashing his head in for what he did!" - **Karen Woodside**

The resources found in secure emotional attachments, which include adaptive experiences, help individuals to navigate certain offenses with minimal impact on their day-to-day activities. However, the vehement nature of some offenses can wreak upheaval in our lives to the extent that daily living is not the same because our functionality becomes impaired. Consequently, life can only go on when we radically change our perspectives!

In some cases of offense, defense mechanisms and a heightened sense of vigilance is deployed by victims. Because of such offenses, anxiety or fear is produced. Anxiety then gives rise to, and understandably so, hesitancy, reticence, and apprehension in venturing out, engaging others, and revealing oneself when it comes to interpersonal relationships.

The reason why such offenses have this kind of impact on us is because they hurt – they wound us! Consequently, the brain works to protect *the self* from future emotional and physical pain.

As emotional beings, we can experience joy, happiness, pleasure, and a sense of wellbeing. But our affect/emotional spectrum does not stop there. We are also able to experience sadness, fear, anger, and a sense that all is not well. All of these emotions play a critical role in our humanity, as well as in our survivability and adaptability during our sojourn on planet Earth.

So, offenses have the capacity to hurt us: But why? Maybe the context of a marriage can help us once again. Picture a newly wedded couple. They open up to each other in every way. As each spouse sees more of the other, each, in turn, reveals more of self. They experience core affects or inner emotions in greater and deepening intimacy because each spouse is taking the risk and becoming more and more vulnerable to the other. The "I love you," and accompanying affectionate behavior continue to flow as their sexual expressions provide for them, yet another means to deepen their intimacy.

There is a sense of companionship, as the couple moves as one to meet or fulfill financial goals and other objectives. When each objective is met, there is a sense of accomplishment, which, for each spouse, further underscores the value of the relationship. There is also a sense of trust, as each spouse believes, that the other has their wellbeing or interests at heart. Additionally, there is a sense of security shared by the spouses because of their pristine trust.

Such a context offers an admirable and ideal situation for a marriage, but soon, an offense in the relationship surfaces. You are not surprised at the arrival of the inevitable (the offensive action), right? Let us call this offense a vehement one in that the husband, sadly, is discovered to be in an extra-marital affair. The wife is stunned by the news and, consequently, loses functionality in her day-to-day activities. She is hurt deeply, emotionally!

It hurts because she had taken the risk, became vulnerable, and revealed her inner and most intimate self to her husband, yet she was violated. The emotional pain is present, and she feels disappointed because the trust that she had reposed in her husband was desecrated. She now sees that he does not have her wellbeing at heart for her trust was devalued and disregarded. There was not a reciprocation of the goodwill that she had extended to her covenantal partner. She feels pain because the sense of companionship that she thought she had was a façade. And because she lost the ideal, she had found in her husband, the pain of the offense, understandably, is now her reality.

The Brain Remembers

The neurobiology of our brains is in constant motion, providing new memory networks and representations that reflect the experiences that we encounter daily. We must also consider that the brain functions to protect *the self* and aids in the healthy functionality of an individual through their adaptive processes. When an individual is in danger, brain functions engage the person somatically, or bodily, through the activation of the fight, flight, or freeze responses, all geared towards the preservation of *the self*. For instance, an encounter with a hornets' nest might activate the flight response of an individual because memory pathways helped the person to consciously recall that a prior experience with a hornet was not pleasant at all, but it was extremely painful. Through this example, we can understand one of the benefits of the brain's function, which helps us to remember, and because of our memory capacity, we can adapt as we go through life's experiences.

Such a capacity comes with the free association process of the brain; it can link one experience with another. This free association can be explained by what I call, "The Miller Effect." If you were to exclaim to me, "Miller ran out of the house!" It would be as if my brain pulled open a drawer in the "Millers' filing cabinet" of my mind so that I can go into the free association zone with the view of trying to find a context for your statement. Is it Elder William Miller? Is it his nephew, Shane Miller? Is it Sean Miller, of my high school days? Or is it the dog, called Miller, who belonged to one member of my cohort, during my Marriage and Family Therapy training? Other variables in our context must be considered in order for me to determine which Miller you are talking about. Therefore, there is a need for the brain's free association!

"The Miller Effect" helps us to understand why it is difficult for us to completely forget a particular offense. The brain acts like a massive storage facility for memories that are ready to be accessed. It even stores the memory of an offense like other experiences. Therefore, memory of an offense can easily come to the fore of our consciousness, through the brain's free association, triggered by a word, scent, sound, or a scene.

Indeed, memory is a wonderful capacity that the Creator has blessed us with. I can recall pleasant memories of my childhood that include shooting marbles and going "rambling" through the bushes with my playmates looking for "coco-plums." The memory of my first vehicle, a 1985 Dodge 600, adds to these pleasant experiences.

Other constituents of my pleasant memories include: my day of gladness, when I became one with a woman who is beautiful, inside and out, in the covenant of marriage; the birth of my first-born son, who I could see now (through my mind's eyes), with his tiny feet up in the air getting ready to cry when the nurse brought him to the door of the nursery so that I could see him for the first time; the arrival of my second and third born sons, who brought with them inexpressible delight; and, a wonderful botanical infusion I experienced during my visit to the beautiful island of Dominica, in the Caribbean. Really, I can go on and on delineating more of the constituents of my pleasant memories from relaxing walks near a cool beach to spiritually enriching times of fellowship with the Creator's people.

However, our brains also store unpleasant memories. You can recall some of them, right? For me, I can remember crying while pulling on my mother's dress, when I was going into grade one for the first time. I probably was experiencing some form of separation anxiety.

Then there was a time when I was forced by my mother to go to my father's food-store to collect some groceries. "What was so unpleasant about that?" you may ask. Well, at the time of the incident, I was around the age of twelve and had only recently been made aware that I had a father. From my tender vantage point, I was going on a mission towards a stranger. Looking back at the situation, it is conceivable that, while she dealt with an issue involving my father, my mother might have used me as some kind of "pawn" in the matter.

As unpleasant and painful as some of my memories may have been, others have experienced far greater disturbances in their lives where intense emotional pain, as in the case of a violent rape, have caused their brains to activate the process of dissociation. In this phenomenon, the brain functions biologically to disconnect the traumatized individual from the emotional and physical pain of the moment so that they are able to endure the unpleasant situation. The brain, therefore, functions as a survival agent on the individual's behalf.

However, while dissociation plays a critical role in the coping and survival modes of emotionally distressed and traumatized individuals, as indicated above, there is still a registering of the event by the brain.

In such cases, while emotions may not exist consciously in the memory of an individual who is traumatized, yet they do exist, unprocessed and fragmented. These fragmented emotions can continue to have an impact on the lives and functionality of those traumatized. Sometimes they manifest themselves in parts of the body through neurological sensations or psychosomatic pain (psychological pain that finds its way in some part of the body).

In a real sense, the body "keeps the score" even though there is dissociation regarding the traumatic experience. Fortunately, the field of psychotherapy can help traumatized individuals work towards processing their unconscious vehement affects or emotions, even as they may be expressed bodily. In other words, through the manifested psychological sensations in parts of the body, therapists can still help individuals identify the accompanying emotions attached to such sensations along with their unconscious memories. Covert emotions then become overt. And because these unconscious feelings/emotions become conscious, they can be processed or re-contextualized. Consequently, better emotional health and functionality is attained by the individual.

By understanding the brain's memory functions and its role in helping to preserve traumatized individuals, even as this may result in unprocessed emotions and their impact on the body, we are provided with a biologically based explanation for the hurt involved in certain offenses. The freshness of an offensive memory recall and trauma's impact on the mind and body contributes significantly to the mental pain and hurt!

Intrusion on Our Rights

I once read a news story that described how a woman was kidnapped by a pair of criminals, a male, and a female. The pair initially invited the woman to their residence. However, when she wanted to leave, she was prevented from doing so. She was later gagged and beaten by her abductors. The male of the criminal pair also raped the woman repeatedly. Fortunately, she was released after a few days. She subsequently contacted the authorities, and they were able to arrest the uncaring and brutal perpetrators.

The above account also helps us to see why offenses can be very hurtful. The woman did not invite the harm that she suffered into her life; individuals who disregarded her person and violated her rights perpetrated it against her.

Sadly, there are individuals in our world who, without compassion, care or regard for their fellow human beings, be they infants or the elderly, are unwilling to accord them the respect and rights that they deserve. Scripture sheds light on the hearts of such individuals:

> But realize this, that in the last days difficult times will come. For men will be lovers of self, lovers of money, boastful, arrogant, revilers, disobedient to parents, ungrateful, unholy, unloving, irreconcilable, malicious gossips, without self-control, brutal, haters of good, treacherous, reckless, conceited, lovers of pleasure rather than lovers of God...(2 Timothy 3:1-4).

More than helping us to see the hearts of individuals that give rise to offenses, like those perpetrated against the woman mentioned above, these verses reveal how much man has fallen short of the ideal of the Creator's intent for the human experience.

The pain from an offense arises because, as offended individuals, we did not give consent to the perpetrator who somehow garnered the fortitude, breached the boundaries of our private and sacred space, and plundered, desecrated, ruined, sabotaged, and discounted the thing that we hold near and dear to us, in that which surrounds us and is attached to our person.

Intrusion is one thing, but seduction is another, yet both can lead to an offense. The perpetrator, who offends through seduction, is not as overt. Rights are often violated within the context of appeal and corrupted trust. This is seen clearly in the cases of young children who are lured by adults, through the promise of material things and a false sense of trust, into inappropriate sexual experiences and relationships. Sadly, it is often familial relations, which provide the ties where such exploitive improprieties and offenses fester.

The Creator's Hurt

Our profile of hurt, which comes through an offense, is not complete if we fail to factor in the hurt that the Creator experiences when He is offended. But how do we measure such hurt? Again, the Scriptures help us! Individuals who have entered a right covenantal relationship with their Creator, and then walk contrary to the tenets of such a covenant by embracing behavior that displeases Him, are described as adulterous: "You adulteresses, do you not know that friendship with the world is hostility toward God? Therefore, whoever wishes to be a friend of the world makes himself an enemy of God" (James 4:4).

Are you intrigued as I am, why the designation "You adulteresses…" and not "You thieves…" or "You slanderers…?" "You adulteresses…" reveal the kind of relationship that the Creator sees Himself as having with His people – a covenantal one, akin to marriage. Since this is the case, He requires His people to hold true to the expectations that accompany such a relationship.

Do you remember the young newlyweds mentioned earlier? How, given the ideal situation, each spouse had companionship, openness, intimacy, security, and a sense of accomplishment? The same can be said about the relationship that the Creator has with His people.

One can even see the risk and vulnerability (the Creator is susceptible to emotional pain) involved in the relationship, especially with the initial extension of the Creator's love: "In this is love, not that we loved God, but that He loved us and sent His son to be the propitiation [*fitting sacrifice*] for our sins" (1 John 4:10). So, when His people breach the covenantal agreement by doing things adverse to the relationship, like the husband in the case of the newlyweds, then they are viewed as adulteresses.

In this adultery, the Creator feels the pain and disappointment that accompanies the infidelity that an individual feels when their spouse acts treacherously against them. It is a cutting emotional pain (yes, the Creator can be and is emotionally vested in His creation and people) that is a consequence of a violation of trust. And it is one that is tantamount to that found in adultery.

The Debt of Offense

As noted earlier, a debt accompanies an offense. The perpetrator of an offense owes the offended. We have examined, a bit, the concept of moral "oughtness" that governs us. In it, human rights and behavioral expectations are protected. When offenses occur, there is a breach in the mutuality of moral "oughtness." In our human experiences, the right way of speaking or acting towards one another is compromised, and consequently, there is a sense of injustice in the offended.

The offended loses something, and the offensive experience, at its core, may "boil down" to a lack of respect on behalf of the perpetrator. The nature of that something may be material, relational, private, or sacred. In such instances, the rights of those offended are not safeguarded; instead, they have been illegitimately taken away. And whether intentional, inadvertent, intrusive, or seductive in nature, the offense gives birth to a debt.

The employer is in debt to the employee who was wrongfully terminated. The company's Chief Executive Officer (CEO) is in debt to his secretary for sexually harassing her in the work environment. Little Johnny's adult male neighbor is in debt to him for betraying his trust and taking advantage of him when he, as an adult, lost propriety and fondled Johnny. An unscrupulous businesswoman is in debt to her business partner for swindling their hard-earned dollars.

Our being in debt can also be directed to our Creator. Since we can offend the Creator, it follows that we can also be in debt to Him. If we embrace unsanctioned behavior before our Creator, we fail to accord Him the respect that He has a right to. When we are resolute in doing things our way, contrary to His way, He then loses given the risk that He has taken and investment made in us.

Is this picture becoming clearer? I am just wondering! The Creator has poured into our existence, so there is a legitimate expectation that He has of us, and that is, He expects us to behave in a certain way towards Him and our fellow human beings. When this expectation is not realized, because of our behavior, which violates His code for our human experience, we find ourselves in debt towards Him.

Offense Emotional Complex

Accompanying the loss experienced in offenses, there is a wide array of core (inner) emotions in those who have been offended. Such emotions are a natural part of our makeup, and conscientiously experiencing them should not be viewed as something abnormal. In fact, core emotions help us to adapt to life's experiences. So, as we become aware of our emotions, "What are we going to do with them?" is a good question to ask. You may feel fearful because of an offense – "What am I going to do with this fear?" is a question you can ask yourself. Fear can drive us to act in keeping with the wellbeing of *the self* and others, or it can negatively immobilize us.

The loss we experience following an offense can also produce in us sadness, anger, and a feeling of regret. In sadness, the absence of something leaves us unhappy. Thus, the laughter and smile we are known for will be noticeably absent. The usual cheerful self is supplanted with a self that is dejected.

We become angry and feel a sense of intense displeasure when someone offends us and violate our rights. There is something that is anger inducing about a thief breaking into our home, causing damage at the entry point, and proceeding to roam freely through our underwear drawers while plundering our belongings. Concomitant with the anger is a desire for justice now that the standard of mutual respect has been broken in the offense.

The feeling of regret can also come with the loss that accompanies an offense. While an offender can feel regret, the offended can also be saddled with the feeling of disappointment. The offended can easily think: "I shouldn't have entered that business partnership"; "I shouldn't have gotten that close to a person that I barely knew"; "I should have taken more time to get to know her before I said, I do"; "I shouldn't…."

An offense perpetrated can cause the individual offended to experience an extended period of sadness or a state of depression. Such a state, although it has garnered debate in the world of psychology as to exactly what it is, has its healthy parameters but can progress to a clinical state. Here, we want to underscore its healthy attributes in our spectrum of natural emotions. Consequently, the loss of something dear and valuable, understandably, can cause one to be sad for a period of time.

As implied in the case of depression, certain emotions that are triggered in the experience of loss, due to an offense, can be very complex.

Another one of such emotions is shame. While it creates negative feelings, it too, has a healthy adaptive dimension. Do you remember the husband that was mortified or embarrassed over his wife's revelation of their bedroom business while they were at dinner with another couple? The husband's feeling of shame led to an adjustment in what he and his wife agreed to divulge in future outings. In this case, the husband's shame served the couple positively.

In feeling shame, we are mortified by the offense, but more than that, the offense, in some instances, is allowed to define us. This is the other dimension of shame: the negative experience is given sweeping, pervasive power that defines our entire being. The offensive and abusive words of the parent are internalized by the child, adopted, and seen as self-defining: "You are no good, just like your no good pa!" is internalized as "I am no good!" by the child.

So, it can easily be understood why this dimension of shame is truly negative. While an individual might be offended, their value or worth surpasses the experience of the offense, no matter how vehement the nature and degree of emotions it produces.

Moreover, the self-description of "I am no good!" runs contrary to the Creator's image of us, His handiwork, according to the psalmist found in Scripture:

> For You formed my inward parts; You wove me in my mother's womb. I will give thanks to You, for I am fearfully and wonderfully made; wonderful are Your works, and my soul knows it very well (Psalm 139:13-14).

The self-description of "I am no good!" is false, especially as we consider the descriptors in "I am fearfully and wonderfully made" and how that each human being can join in with the psalmist and appropriate them.

As we experience an array of emotions as a result of an offense, the Creator also experiences the same. Regarding regret, within the context of the Creator's displeasure and judgment on man long ago, the Scripture speaks:

Then the Lord saw that the wickedness of man was great on the earth, and that every intent of the thoughts of his heart was only evil continually. The Lord was sorry that He had made man on the earth, and He was grieved in His heart. The Lord said, 'I will blot out man whom I have created from the face of the land, from man to animals to creeping things and to birds of the sky; for I am sorry that I have made them (Genesis 6:5-7).

The Creator was sorry and grieved that He had made man because of his improper behavior while he occupied his place in the universe.

Again, man's offense produced an emotion in the Creator, but this time it was anger:

The Lord said to Moses, 'I have seen this people, and behold, they are an obstinate people. Now then let Me alone, that My anger may burn against them and that I may destroy them; and I will make of you a great nation (Exodus 32:9-10).

While this portion of Scripture reveals the Creator's prerogative, to punish an obstinate people, it also reveals His capacity for the core (deep within His being) emotion of anger over the loss He experienced as a result of their offense.

Loss and Unforgiveness

Of special note is the emotion of unforgiveness, which is connected to the loss suffered in an offense. The perpetrator of the offense intruded on our rights as they disregarded our feelings, personal space, and the things that we hold as sacred. Sometimes, because of our intense emotions, particularly anger, that accompany our loss, we are unwilling to forgive the perpetrator. In such an emotional state, we bear a grudge; that is, we maintain ill feelings towards the perpetrator of an offense. There is resentment, characterized by a feeling of bitterness and indignation towards the offending party. Avoidance of the offender can also accompany this emotional state. Because of the injustice, there is malice residing in the hearts or spirits of the offended, and quite often, they seek a payback or revenge for the wrong experienced.

Like offenses, which pervade human relations, unforgiveness can also pervade human relations. The emotion of unforgiveness can exist between family members, as well as in the relationship between employer and employee, or even between neighbors. Unforgiveness can also define the relationship of total strangers. The stranger who jumped the line in the checkout section of the grocery store can be the object of unforgiveness.

Not only is unforgiveness pervasive, but it can also be perpetual in nature. Have you ever heard about family members who have not spoken to one another in years because an offense occurred between them? You might have heard something like this, "My sister, Lorriane, and I have not been on speaking terms for five years now." This may be a marker of the foothold the emotion of unforgiveness has established in the relationship. A twenty-five-year-old grudge held by a father, that toppled what could have been experienced in a meaningful and enriching relationship between he and his son, clearly speaks to the continuity that can be attached to unforgiveness. Unforgiveness can have staying power! Or should I say, "Unforgiveness can be given staying power?"

The emotion of unforgiveness is one of those defensive mechanisms that many of us deploy in order to protect *the self.* But as we will see, it has a negative impact on us as individuals. In a very real sense, unforgiveness perpetuates the hurt found in the offense.

The Toll of Unforgiveness

Allowing the emotion of unforgiveness to influence our person, as well as our lives, is costly. Unforgiveness impacts us psychologically in a huge way. While anger can be the precursor for unforgiveness, unforgiveness can perpetuate anger. So, you have a certain kind of vicious cycle.

Anger, in turn, can skew our judgments. Take, for instance, the statement, "All men are dogs!" It may come from a divorced woman who has been offended, perhaps, by an unfaithful husband. She is angry over the matter and, consequently, she enters a state of bitter unforgiveness. This state leads her to the erroneous position of stereotyping all men as dogs. However, we know that this is not the case! All men are not dogs! Not only is such a view erroneous, but it also has the potential of blinding the woman from the prospect of developing a good and beneficial relationship with a different man.

Not only can those offended be caught up in an anger, unforgiveness, anger cycle, but they can also find themselves in an offense, unforgiveness, offense cycle (*see figures 1 & 2*). Due to the loss and the desire to right the wrong, individuals sometimes take steps to "get even." However, very often, when this is done, another wrong is perpetrated.

Take the case of a news report that revealed the sale of a Nike Air Jordan pair of tennis that went awfully wrong. The report revealed that a family man would typically sell tennis shoes over the Internet, via Craigslist. After arranging to meet a purchaser of one pair of his shoes, an offense occurred: The would-be purchaser pulled out a gun, pointed it in the face of the family man, and robbed him of the tennis shoes that were for sale. The robber even pulled the trigger of the gun, but it jammed. Indeed, this was a traumatic experience for the family man. Video footage showed the robber casually walking away from the scene of the offense and the family man slowly driving off in his SUV.

Moments later, the footage revealed the family man running over, with deadly speed, the robber with his SUV. The robber is seen running away from the encounter, without one of his arms. The authorities eventually held both the family man and the robber for the offenses they perpetrated.

The story above is a tough one to deal with. What would I have done? How would you have handled it? Why did he not follow the robber at a distance and contact the police? It was even suggested in the report that the family man acted out of a state of shock, and certainly, that might have been the case. What do you think?

As we move along in our time together, we will identify some of the ways a sense of balance and justice can be achieved when injustice is perpetrated in certain offenses, and there is disharmony in our mutual moral "oughtness." But for now, the story above reveals how an offense can beget an offense, and the thing that often moves this cycle is unforgiveness.

The psychological burden of unforgiveness does not end at impaired judgments. It can also lead to the perpetuation of sadness, and a clinical state of depression, along with a host of other emotions, which promote fear instead of adaptive tendencies within the individual. Anxiety, which is a type of fear, then becomes the cause for uneasiness and apprehension in relational dealings. There is a real prospect that an individual's functionality can be negatively affected by unforgiveness!

Because of unforgiveness, the energy that would ordinarily be used to create and build us up, in the normal scheme of things, is now deployed assiduously to protect *the self* or it simply meets an unproductive, non-potentiated state, evidenced in a lack of interest, as in the case of clinical depression. Unforgiveness, therefore, can "cage" us in, cutting off our ability and freedom to function to our fullest capacity or potential.

Unforgiveness attracts and maintains the power of others over our lives. It may not seem like we are allowing others to exercise control over us while in the emotional state of unforgiveness, but if we pause and consider this idea for a few minutes, we will be able to see the "controlling strings" of others attached to our lives, like those of a puppeteer to his puppets.

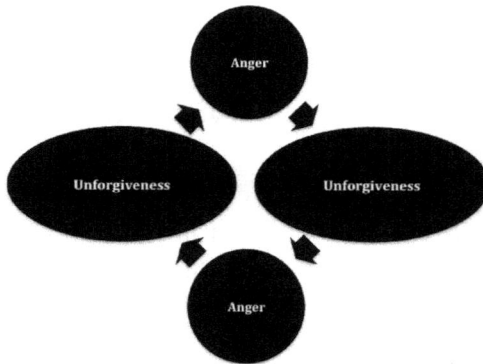

Figure 1 – *The Anger, Unforgiveness, Anger Cycle*

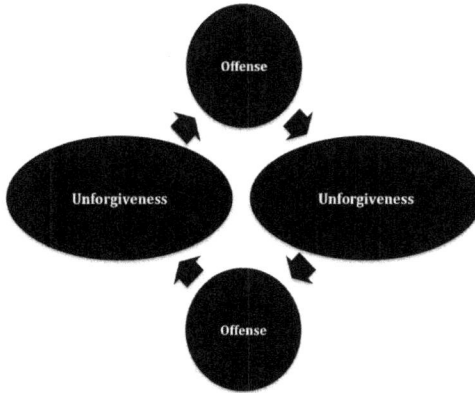

Figure 2 – *The Offense, Unforgiveness, Offense Cycle*

Unforgiveness can also have an adverse effect on our physical health and wellbeing. Studies have linked unforgiveness to cancer, heart attacks, sleep disorders, negative cholesterol levels, anxiety, clinical depression, and high blood pressure. In their study, Charlotte vanOyen Witvliet, et al, found that:

> Although fleeting feelings of unforgiveness may not erode health, more frequent, intense, and sustained unforgiving emotional imagery and behaviors may create physiological vulnerabilities or exacerbate existing problems in a way that erodes health.[6]

The body, because of anger, experiences emotional arousal, and it goes into fight or flight mode. In these states, certain hormones are released for survival purposes, and too much and too long an exposure to such hormones can have an adverse effect on our physical health. We noted earlier how unforgiveness perpetuates the anger.

From Scripture, we find a fitting metaphor that can describe unforgiveness: that is, it is a yoke around the neck. As unforgiveness is described as a yoke here, it can be seen as something that is oppressive and burdensome. Let us take an initial look at the biblical character, Esau. He is the firstborn of Isaac, one of the patriarchs of national and historic Israel and the twin brother of Jacob. Esau and Jacob's relationship did not escape the negative consequences of an offense.

Jacob was part of a plan that his mother concocted, which was designed to deprive his brother Esau, who was the firstborn, of his blessing from their father. Although treacherous and daring in nature, especially, as it involved getting Isaac to believe that Jacob was Esau by utilizing goats' skins, the plan succeeded. But not without the injury and pain of Jacob's offense being registered with Esau:

> Then he said, 'Is he not rightly named Jacob, for he has supplanted me these two times? He took away my birthright, and behold, now he has taken away my blessing'... So Esau bore a grudge against Jacob because of the blessing with which his father had blessed him; and Esau said to himself, 'The days of mourning for my father are near; then I will kill my brother Jacob' (Genesis 27:36-41).

Notice the loss that Esau experienced, in his blessing being taken away, and the emotion of unforgiveness that developed in his heart, bearing a grudge against his brother, Jacob. However, while Scripture reveals his life to be wanting and less than admirable in a few ways – given that he despised his birthright and was unrepentant for a period, as indicated in his plot to kill Jacob – Esau manifested a quality that was and is most admirable. I will develop this quality shortly!

After the treacherous act of Jacob's offense was revealed to Isaac, he uttered a prophetic word to Esau:

> By your sword you shall live, and your brother you shall serve;
> but it shall come about when you become restless, then you
> will break his yoke from your neck (Genesis 27:40).

The above verse of Scripture primarily addresses the nations that descended from both Jacob (historical Israel) and Esau (historical Edom), and it projected Edom's revolt from servitude under and tribute to Israel! However, there is a portion of the verse that is so fitting, as we would take it and apply it to Esau's emotional journey while dealing with the offense that was perpetrated against him by Jacob. That portion of the verse is "...when you become restless, then you will break his yoke from your neck."

The admirable quality that Esau possessed was his ability to move from a state of emotional unforgiveness to forgiveness towards Jacob. In this regard, he was able to break the yoke of unforgiveness from around his neck.

The negative impact of unforgiveness can also adversely affect our relationship with our Creator. For those of us in the human experience that have the Creator as our spiritual Father, it is incumbent upon us to forgive the offenses of others, if we would have our offenses forgiven: "But if you do not forgive others, then your Father will not forgive your transgressions" (Matthew 6:15). One action is contingent upon the other! Unforgiveness then has the capacity to block and disrupt the wholesome relationship that we can have with our Creator.

What is also implied in the above verse is we have a choice. We can choose whether to allow unforgiveness to shape or not shape our thought processes and behavior. Notwithstanding the emotional pain or trauma, and the incapacity of some to choose during an offense, amidst the psychological and emotional hurt, we still have to make the choice to forgive, or not forgive, the one who has offended us. Are you still buckled up?

For further deliberation…

1. Why is trust failure so hurtful?

2. How is it that any offense perpetrated against an individual can never define them?

3. Can the Creator really lose His investment in us as human beings?

4. How much of a yoke is unforgiveness?

5. Is there actually a choice in the midst of unforgiveness?

I Forgive

Chapter Three

The Option of Forgiving!

*"I am so angry at my husband, but I know that God would want me to forgive him." - **Karen Woodside***

We have just seen how unforgiveness can negatively impact our lives from a physiological, psychological, functional, and relational perspective. While the yoke of unforgiveness can be borne, because of its oppressive and burdensome qualities for those who carry it, it really becomes a means of self-sabotage. Individuals can do great injury to themselves if they allow the emotion of unforgiveness to take root and fester in their lives.

Therefore, I want to call your attention to a viable alternative – *forgiving the offender*. It is an alternative to the yoke of unforgiveness because it can significantly reduce or eliminate the self-sabotage and lift the psychological burden from an individual's life. It helps to restore the vital energy needed to become creative and productive in a state of healthy functionality. Forgiving the offender is the admirable quality that Esau exhibited towards his brother, Jacob.

You may ask, "Esau forgave, but what about my justice?" Before we look further at what is involved with forgiving an offender, we must understand what forgiving an individual is not. As we do so, I will also reveal a perspective on justice and how it is achieved when there is a breach in our mutual moral "oughtness."

Clarity in Forgiving!

Dr. Laura Schlessinger, in her book, *10 Stupid Things Women Do To Mess Up Their Lives,* introduced the concept of "Stupid Forgiving."[7] I really appreciate her work and the way she addresses the psychological concerns attached to poor decisions individuals make. So much so, that I ordered three more of her books. I must admit, though, I was a little disappointed that Dr. Schlessinger did not develop the concept of "Stupid Forgiving" more than she did. Maybe, she felt that "Stupid Forgiving" is self-explanatory!

Nevertheless, I thank Dr. Schlessinger for the concept because, for me, it reveals that there is a particular responsibility that is inherent within extending forgiveness. This is not to say that it should not be extended. On the contrary! Rather, as it is extended, it must not be done arbitrarily, that is, without careful consideration of its accompaniments and the context within which it is offered.

For instance, re-establishment of a relationship is a possible outcome when the offended forgives the offender, but if such an offender tends to become physically abusive, displaying fits of rage in the relationship, reinstatement should be placed on hold until help is found and received. Such a position would preserve the wellbeing of all concerned and help to advance the positive path of extending forgiveness within a positive context.

Forgiving an offender should be seen to be keeping company with justice, repentance, help sought, behavioral differences, professional help, legal issues, and victim protection, among other factors. Therefore, the process needs to take on a systematic quality, where consideration is given to all that is connected to it.

Reconciliation and Its Accompaniments

To forgive an offender does not mean that reconciliation is automatic or even possible in all cases; to forgive the offender is not the same as to be reconciled with them. The reality is that certain offenses have the potential of violently causing an upheaval in our lives, whereby things could never be the same again. The mold that shaped the contours of life is broken through the offense: "She betrayed my trust when she slept with another man, so I don't want anything to do with her anymore." The hard reality, in some cases, is that there may never be reconciliation or reinstatement because of the severity of the offense. Still, reconciliation remains a viable option that is contingent upon some critical considerations.

Several factors influence reconciliation. The availability of the offender is one of these factors. We might have lost contact with individuals who have offended us; they might be deceased or may have moved to another part of the world. Death, particularly about family relations, has made it impossible for many to fulfill their intentions of being reconciled with their offenders. This moves to the fore, a sense of urgency and diligence about striving after it, should reconciliation be potentially possible.

Then there is the willingness of both the offended and the offender who desire reconciliation. Notwithstanding the nobility attached to reconciliation, the desire for the restoration of a relationship must reside in the hearts of all concerned with the offense. And as much as the offended or the offender may want and make attempts towards reconciliation, it cannot be forced out of individuals; all parties must want it.

We should be mindful of the fact that reconciliation must be the desire of those concerned with the offense. If any one of them seek to make conciliatory efforts towards the other, but the same is not reciprocated, the individual making the effort should be assured that they are acting commendably and nobly while moving towards the ideal, in terms of the harmony that beautifies the human experience.

Safety is another factor that should influence reconciliation. We know and have heard horror stories of physical, sexual, and mental abuses, which have had a traumatic impact on those experiencing such offenses. Being apprised of such happenings brings to the fore the safety of those abused. The news and revelation of the violation of our tender ones (children), who are too naive and susceptible to ward off perpetrators who would exploit them sexually, invoke within us a sense of anger and bewilderment, which moves us to protect them. When we learn of a wife who has been disrespected and battered by her husband, we know that something is wrong, and we express interest in the woman's safety and protection.

These accounts help us to appreciate that before the subject of reconciliation can be broached, there need to be a significant change in the context(s) within which the offense(s) occurred. And not just any change but change that will promote or optimize the wellbeing of all concerned.

Reconciliation is a bit different with the Creator. When He forgives an offender, it results in the restoration or reinstatement of a wholesome relationship and peace with Him. However, for the offender to experience the Creator's forgiveness and reconciliation, there are additional considerations one must be aware of and follow. We will identify them in our time together, so keep reading!

A Perspective on Excuse and Approval

Forgiving an offender is not making an excuse for their wrong. If there is to be a meaningful and positive change in any negative situation, there must be an acknowledgement of its reality! In the case of the alcoholic husband and father, if he is to get the help that he needs, he must acknowledge that he has a problem. But not him alone, family members must recognize his drinking or abuse of alcohol for what it is, a problem. His wife should not make excuses for him, thus, enabling him in his offensive habit and behavior. Sadly, sometimes, it takes a crisis for the alcoholic to wake up, acknowledge his problem, and seek help.

There should not be any cloaking of the offense. Behavior that disrupts or destroys relationships, cause mayhem in our societies, and produces blight on our human experience, must be identified, called out, and marked for what it is – *offensive*. Actually, if there is to be an extension of forgiveness and receipt of the same, all concerned must admit that an offense has taken place.

Similarly, forgiving the offender is not approving the wrong. This point deserves special attention, especially in our world where there is a blurring of the line about what is wholesome and what is not. For some, psychological damage and deceit have caused them to "miscategorize" the offensive behavior, giving validation to it.

Consequently, according to a publicized finding that was broadcast on the radio, a great portion of the population of a country see nothing wrong with men who maltreat their wives or girlfriends. The finding also revealed that some women expect their men to use a "little force" to keep them in line. It is likely that such a perspective will result in a culture that supports multiple incidences of physical and sexual abuse.

In societies today, moral lines may be blurred; however, in forgiving an offender, the offense must be identified, acknowledged, and repudiated.

The Offender's Worthiness

What about the offender's worthiness? Is forgiving an offender hinged on their merit? Perhaps, we have heard this promise: "If you forgive me this time, I promise, I will never do it again." While behavior modification, or the lack thereof, is a consideration when extending forgiveness, the process is not exclusively attached to it.

The efforts of the offender, to make redress, is commendable and constitutes part of what I refer to as the fertile ground for extending forgiveness (a concept to be developed later). However, extending forgiveness can move forward without the offender's efforts.

Forgiving and Forgetting

We have been introduced to "The Miller Effect," a phenomenon that seeks to explain the memory and free-associative functions of our brain. The brain can "pull a memory file" when it is triggered by a scent, voice, name, scene, musical note, or a certain ambiance, so it is tough to forget, outright. Notwithstanding degenerative abnormalities and injury, which may occur in the neurological makeup of our brains, we will remember the offense and the offender.

Therefore, for us, as human beings, extending forgiveness is not equivalent to forgetting the offense, which has received representation as a memory pattern in the neurobiological makeup of our brains.

Is Justice Precluded in Extending Forgiveness?

To forgive the offender does not mean that justice is negated, or a debt payment withheld. Human rights and dignity should be respected, and when certain offenses occur, there should be the expected subsequent righting of the wrongs. There are consequences that are attached to our behaviors. Some of these consequences are punitive in nature. When the mutual moral "oughtness" has been breached, the offensive behavior must be checked. The value of the offended must be safeguarded and recompense given to them. Justice must be meted out!

So, in a very real sense, out of justice, offenders may find themselves behind bars, serving some lengthy prison term, or even in jeopardy of losing their lives because of some terrible offense. Such a view is not incongruent with forgiving an offender because both justice and forgiveness can coexist.

There are two entities that function in helping to right the wrong by providing justice. We have seen that we can enter the cycle of offense, unforgiveness, and offense, as we take matters into our own hands when we are violated. Fortunately, this does not have to be the case, as the Creator, by His providential working, has provided an entity, in the governing authority, to act punitively on His behalf:

> For rulers are not a cause of fear for good behavior, but for evil. Do you want to have no fear of authority? Do what is good, and you will have praise from the same; for it is a minister of God to you for good. But if you do what is evil, be afraid; for it does not bear the sword for nothing; for it is a minister of God, an avenger who brings wrath on the one who practices evil (Romans 13:3-4).

The governing bodies have been vested with the authority to punish, require the payment of the debt, mete out justice, or stop the offending perpetrator with the assurance that they are acting on the Creator's behalf. I believe that many governments do not fully function in this authority. As a result, the fear factor that could work proactively in helping to curb the-would-be offender's action is not optimized. Nevertheless, recourse can be found in the governing authority that should function to address the injustice or debt inherent in applicable offenses.

The people who belong to the Creator are encouraged to respect and use such recourse and not take matters into their own hands:

> Never take your own revenge, beloved, but leave room for the wrath of God, for it is written, 'Vengeance is Mine, I will repay,' says the Lord. 'But if your enemy is hungry, feed him, and if he is thirsty, give him a drink; for in so doing you will heap burning coals on his head.' Do not be overcome by evil but overcome evil with good (Romans 12:19-21).

Do you see the dilemma Karen Woodside found herself in? On the one hand, she wanted to take her own vengeance, but on the other, she knew that the Creator required a different action (one that was unlike hers). Such tension has a positive side attached to it! It nudges, and motivates, towards a noble course! Also, along with helping an individual on the path that is acceptable to the Creator, it assists in lifting the yoke of unforgiveness.

"Never take your own revenge" brings into focus the non-retaliatory dimension of extending forgiveness. From a natural perspective, the loss occurred through the offense, so there is a desire to personally "settle the score" and seek a payback.

There is a desire to withhold your goodwill to teach them a lesson out of a "get even" spirit. There is monitoring of the time and place for the ideal opportunity to strike back with deadly force for maximum destructive impact on the offender. However, such a natural perspective is inconsistent with the process of extending forgiveness.

In our world today, as in times past, there are some punitive offenses that have escaped the attention of governmental authorities. Consequently, some perpetrators of egregious offenses go, as it were, scot-free on this side of the universe. This understanding brings us to the other side of the coin: While extending forgiveness does not preclude justice, the process can take place without it. Because of the yoke of unforgiveness, it becomes appropriate to forgive even though the debt has not been paid or justice mete out.

Rest assured, while injustices through offenses have escaped the authorities on this side, they have not escaped the notice of the Creator's ultimate authority, and He will require the debt at the hands of the perpetrators of offenses:

> The conclusion, when all has been heard, is: fear God and keep His commandments, because this applies to every person. For God will bring every act to judgment, everything which is hidden, whether it is good or evil (Ecclesiastes 12:13-14).

Because the Creator is concerned about our relational dynamics, with regard to one another, He has taken upon Himself the responsibility of righting every wrong, in thorough fashion, when those within the human experience become accountable to Him: "For we must all appear before the judgment seat of Christ, so that each one may be recompensed for his deeds in the body, according to what he has done, whether good or bad" (2 Corinthians 5:10).

"Only God Can Forgive Him!"

When we hear such remarks like, "I have not totally forgiven her" or "I can't forgive him," what is implied is an inability, on the speaker's behalf, to extend forgiveness and to do so entirely. Yet, not only are we capable of fully participating in this process of extending forgiveness, there is a need to share in the act of forgiving the offender! Moreover, there is a Divine expectation for the offended to do so!

We have noted the involvement of others, the governing authorities and the Creator, and their roles with regard to offenses. However, with all sensitivity to the gravity of the offense, the offended has a responsibility too! Because of the hurt the offended has experienced, there is a need for them to at least explore a bit or seek out what is entailed in this process of extending forgiveness.

By extending forgiveness, those offended have an opportunity to experience the restoration of a broken relationship. Where there is war, there can be peace, and where there is the absence of the ideal harmony, there can be relational accord.

However, it must be borne in mind that extending forgiveness is primarily about the offended: their relationship with the Creator, their cognitive health; their functionality; and, their general wellbeing. The experience of inter-relational harmony, because of the extension of forgiveness, can be seen as the "icing on the cake."

To Forgive: To What?

The individual, who extends forgiveness, although difficult at times, is projecting a certain kind of nobility. Not only is nobility attached to this individual, but also strength. He or she needs internal strength to navigate the many emotions that an offense brings, painful and difficult as they may be, and settle on one that may not be so popular or easily attained. In fact, extending forgiveness manifests functional strength in an individual as he or she processes the non-trivial in the offense(s). Really, the person who exhibits such strength must be commended!

The emotional process of extending forgiveness is different from the emotions generated from unforgiveness, which perpetuates the hurt in an already broken relationship. And unlike the offense perpetrated, extending forgiveness is aligned with the positive marks found in the human experience.

From the vantage point of the offended, extending forgiveness is a good thing. From the vantage point of the offender, it is a good thing, especially, as forgiveness is received by the individual who perpetrated an offense. As indicated earlier, relationships can be positively impacted through the process of extending forgiveness; therefore, it is a process that can be described as a good, honorable, and excellent thing to do. Did I just sing the praises of extending forgiveness?

Extending forgiveness means love can find traction towards another human being. I recently heard a remix of the popular song, "What the World Needs Now Is Love," by a cross-section of artists, including Dionne Warwick, who can be credited for partly popularizing it. Well, extending forgiveness will allow us to add to the measure of love realized in the universe because we understand that to forgive is in harmony with love.

There is more to this understanding that extending forgiveness is congruent with love; as it provides the opportunity for an individual to act out of love, it also gives the person the opportunity to take on a quality that belongs to the Creator. Through this act of love or affection, that is, extending forgiveness, one is sharing in an attribute that defines our Creator: "The one who does not love does not know God, for God is love" (1 John 4:8).

Notwithstanding the nobility that is attached to extending forgiveness, the process can be misunderstood. We have seen a bit of what extending forgiveness is not, so now we will endeavor to understand what is involved in the process. We start by refocusing on the responsibility that the offended has within the context of the offense. Yes, those offended can assume responsibility for extending forgiveness to their offenders! This responsibility points to and is attached to volition or the exercise of the offended free will; in most instances, this has not been diminished through the offense. Therefore, extending forgiveness is an emotional journey that stems from our decision-making capacity – we decide to forgive!

The decision to forgive is a conscientious one characterized by intentionality. It is a decision that ought to emanate from the inner self or the heart of the individual making it. Therefore, the decision to forgive should not be made under false pretenses, especially if one is going to be accorded the benefits that it brings to the offended. Forgiveness articulated through the words, "I forgive you," should reflect equally the emotional state of the inner dimensions of the individual. There should be integrity attached to the utterance!

The ability to make decisions is an awesome privilege that the Creator has bestowed upon us. We are quite familiar with such a privilege. We decide which cereal we want to eat this week from the copious choices we find in the cereal aisle of the local food store. We decide where we are going to spend our vacation each year: Will it be in Hawaii, our local area, or in Florida? We exercise the capacity to make decisions every day, so it should come as no surprise that we can decide to extend forgiveness to those who have offended us.

The Process

I have been referring to the act of extending forgiveness as a process that comprises a series of actions. A few critical steps can be considered, as individuals are brought to the point where they decide to pardon an offender, thus releasing them from their debt. Such steps in the process point the offended in the direction of the ideal, where it is possible and appropriate, of relational harmony. This ideal reflects the Creator's intent for the human experience, especially for His people: "If possible, so far as it depends on you, be at peace with all men" (Romans 12:18).

For some who have been offended, the process can begin with gaining an understanding of the oppressive weight the emotional yoke of unforgiveness has had on their lives. It may be that sleep is disturbed, as there is a constant cognitive rumination on the offender's action(s).

Recognizing this, the offended may know that they are not functioning in their usual way or self because the situation is actually "getting to them." Cognizant of such a weight, the subsequent action in the process may lead them to a conscious decision to extend forgiveness to their offenders, because they do not want the situation to control them any longer.

Regarding others who have been offended, the process may need to begin with them obtaining acute care through an alliance with a therapist in a clinical setting. In such cases, the traumatic impact of offenses can be worked through. The offended is helped to a place of empathy (which is characterized by having a participatory understanding of the feelings of another) towards their offender(s).

This empathy allows the offended to explore the context within which the offender functions. As the offended examines and notices deficits (emotional, spiritual, environmental, physical, and/or otherwise) in the offender's life, compassion can find traction, which subsequently leads to the bestowal of grace, a concept that we will explore soon. Empathy, therefore, forms a "bridge" that the offended needs to cross towards conscientiously deciding to extend forgiveness to their offenders.

For the traumatized offended, the formation of empathy comes through "restorying," reframing, or re-contextualizing the traumatic hurtful experiences. Through re-contextualization, the emotions of trauma and hurtful memories are experienced from a new perspective – our cognitive processes receive a "makeover." This "makeover," in re-contextualization, does not trivialize the offense, but rather, it provides a different perspective of the offense, resulting in a change of emotions towards the perpetrator. Re-contextualization then is critical to the action of extending forgiveness.

Notwithstanding the challenges that are encountered in the process of forgiving offenders, it is hoped that this work would help to inform the re-contextualization exercise of those offended, whether with "large trauma" or "small trauma," and bring them to a state of empathy where they would then find it easier to forgive (*see figure 3*).

I intend to develop the principles that will help the offended experience re-contextualization, as their focus is brought to the concept of extending forgiveness. But first, we must understand that the action of substitution is a significant factor in the process. I am sure you are aware of the act of substitution when one thing or person is placed in the position of another. For example, a substitute teacher takes over a Biology class after the regular teacher becomes ill.

Similarly, we can substitute one emotion for another as well as restrict certain emotions in our lives, along with the negative actions to which they may lead. We can exert a measure of control over our emotions! This is in harmony with Scripture: "He who is slow to anger is better than the mighty, and he who rules his spirit, than he who captures a city" (Proverbs 16:32).

Emotional substitution can and needs to be found at every juncture of the process of extending forgiveness. It forms a kind of pillar on which the re-contextualization phase for the offended is built. New perspectives, in this phase, have a better opportunity of making a difference when they rest on a positive set of emotions.

Empathy also needs a set of positive emotions to rest upon, such as compassion and tenderness and not unkindness, nestled in bitterness.

The decision to extend forgiveness also reflects a shift from the negative emotions of the offense. And inherent with the actual extending of forgiveness, which is an emotional process itself, we have an emotional supplanting that takes place where a disposition of liberation occupies the place where resentment once rested. So, travel the length and breadth of the process of extending forgiveness, and you will encounter this emotional substitution.

Figure 3 – The Process of Extending Forgiveness.

Goodwill towards the offender is now substituted for a personal desire to get even or seek payback, in a grudge. With such goodwill, there is a desire to see the offender flourish, progress, and come into what they can be in full potentiality within their humanity. There is no delight in the offender's downfall, and neither is there the desire to place impediments in the way of their success. The desire to "fuel" or "fan" hurt, in malice, is supplanted with that of wanting to help and heal. In short, there is a genuine desire for the offender to prosper.

Additionally, human affection is substituted for hatred. Care must be exercised here! There should always be an aversion to the wrongs that breach our mutual moral "oughtness!" However, there is a line of demarcation between the offense and the offender. The offense is not the offender! He or she is still responsible for their action(s) and the resulting consequences; yet, beyond the offense, the individual can still become the object of our human affection. This love sees the person as the Creator intended, with the capacity for good, possessing unique attributes that can make unique contributions to the human experience, even after an offense.

The release is substituted for keeping a record of the offender's debt. You might have heard the saying, "I will forgive you, but I am not going to forget what you have done!" Do you hear the contradiction in that statement? Such a stance implies that there is a conscientious effort made by the offended to hold on to the offensive behavior or debt of the offender. In this, the offense is nursed, kept alive and in view for easy referencing. Why the record keeping in this instance? Possibly, because it is a part of a personal payback or revenge plot, that can be executed at an opportune time.

However, in substituting release for the debt, the offense is removed from the offender's account by the offended. There is a conscientious "erasing" or "blotting" out of the debt. The image of a mortgage being burned comes to mind. In this instance, however, the burning is not preceded by a successful repayment of the debt in timely monthly installments by the debtor; rather, in a gracious act and in illustrative language, it is preceded by a group of friends coming together to help the widow of another friend retire a debt that she could not repay. This is so typical of offenses that are perpetrated against us; so often, the losses are so invaluable and incalculable that to think that an offender can actually repay a debt is inconceivable.

So, there is a "burning of the debt" of the offender in our cognitive processes; maybe, it would be helpful to write the debt on a piece of paper and literally burn it. Consequently, the offender is viewed as if they had never committed the offense. In this view, suitable behavior follows by the offended and, where possible and appropriate, the offender is treated in a way consistent with the offense having not been committed. Are you still buckled up?

The work of substituting one emotion for another, in this process of extending forgiveness, includes substituting grace for vindictiveness. Grace or favor is an interesting word with enormous implications, particularly, as it relates to the Creator. You might have heard of the multifaceted, indescribable grace of God. The Creator's grace has many facets that apply to the physical and spiritual dimensions of our existence here on earth; indeed, it is a splendid thing! While grace is consistent with the image and character of the Creator, human beings are also able to handle and apply it, particularly with regard to those who have offended us.

Vindictiveness points to a strong desire to get even, and we know that the offended possessing such an attitude is harming themselves. But extending grace toward the offender is a viable emotional alternative to vindictiveness. As the offender is released from the debt and viewed as though they did not offend, they become the object of favor or grace by the offended.

Why should grace be offered? Not only does the offering of grace ensure that the offended does not respond in kind (a place where treachery meets nobility), but it also points to a regard for the weaknesses of both the offended and the offender. Can I say it? I think I am going to: "My offender can use some grace today because I may need some tomorrow."

Anger or vexation, which can be manifested in hostility, is supplanted by peace in this emotional substitution. We have seen our anger, unforgiveness, anger cycle, and how, by entering it, the offended can perpetuate harm to themselves and others. Anger, when left unchecked, has resulted in many having to deal with uncalculated consequences, including prison time, loss of a job, loss of health, loss of dignity, and even loss of life.

While the offender can benefit from the peaceful disposition of the offended, it should be understood that such a disposition or mindset primarily holds advantages for the offended. A peaceful disposition towards an offender makes way for appropriate behavior when an offense occurs.

Regret, post the offense, is absent because of this peaceful mindset. So, you do not hear, "I should have thought it through before I acted." In the presence of turmoil, a peaceful mindset benefits the offended – it can help to reduce or even eliminate the emotional pain of the offense. In other words, through a peaceful mindset, the progressive wounding path of the offense is curtailed.

"How can I have peace when my world has been turned upside down?" you may ask. It is not always easy to turn from anger to a peaceful mindset. Especially, if you have been traumatize by a robber who entered your personal space and violated your human dignity by placing a gun to your head, threatening your life over material items. Yet, it is possible!

Becoming mindful of our emotional state when we are offended can help us to initiate the necessary pause that is in keeping with emotional substitution. This is doable because, if you recall, we can exercise a measure of control over our emotions. So, the offended being aware that they are angry because of an offense is a good thing; now, they can decide what to do next with the emotion of anger.

In substituting peace for anger, we very well can offer a blessing instead of a curse. In harmony with this emotional substitution, we can conscientiously determine that we will allow our spirits and minds to be pervaded with tranquility and mental calm, even in the face of some of the most difficult offenses perpetrated against us. This is not to suggest that we are emotionally cold or unfeeling; rather, I am suggesting that we, the offended, can hold the reins of our emotional state, and determine what we allow to impact it, even as certain offenses are considered.

Concurrent with our makeup, as human beings, is our ability to choose. This ability can also be exercised over the emotions we allow to pervade our cognitive processes. Consequently, the complex negative emotions attached to an offense, which have the capacity to harm us beyond the offense, can be supplanted with an equally complex set of positive emotions that promote healing and wholeness, as we go through this process of extending forgiveness (*see figure 4*).

We will now shift to the principles that can help us, the offended, gain a different perspective towards forgiving our offenders, as we experience re-contextualization. I want to provide you with information that could help you to see things differently or view the offense from a different vantage point.

Remember, to see things differently will be of significant benefit to you, the offended. Of course, it may be that you have already begun to see things differently, yet I want to go further and provide you, not exhaustively, with a fuller picture of what is involved in this work of forgiving an offender. I hope that you are still buckled up!

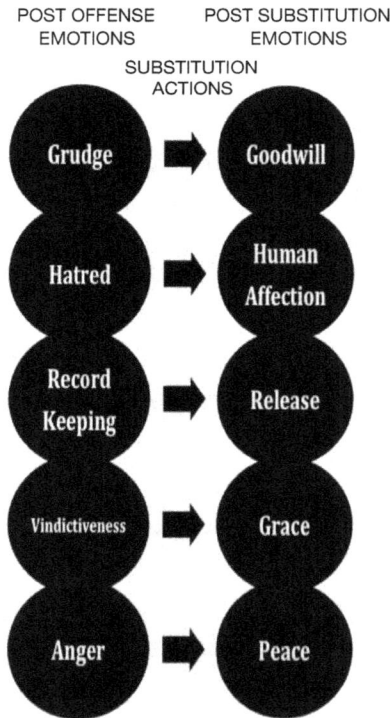

Figure 4 – *The Work of Emotional Substitution*

For further deliberation…

1. In forgiving an offender, should other considerations be made? Why or why not?

2. When offended, we often think about justice, the righting of the wrong; how might we feel less anxious about it?

3. Do you agree that extending forgiveness is primarily an act for the offended? Why or why not?

4. How might we ensure that our actions are in harmony with the words, "I forgive you?"

5. Extending forgiveness is a process, but it is still subjected to our decision-making capacity; do you agree? Why or why not?

6. Is it asking too much, in forgiving offenders, to want to see them prosper?

I Forgive

Chapter Four

The Company of The Offended

Moving forward, the task before us is to build a foundation that re-contextualization can rest upon. Why do we need such a foundation? So, that those offended can be helped with the work of emotional substitution. "Wait a minute!" you may exclaim. "Didn't you explain earlier that emotional substitution helps the offended move towards re-contextualization, a major part of the process of extending forgiveness?" You are right! However, you should also recall that I pointed out that emotional substitution is present at every step in the process of extending forgiveness. And so, as emotional substitution helps re-contextualization, re-contextualization helps emotional substitution. Therefore, we have the re-contextualization, emotional substitution, re-contextualization cycle, in which each visits and impacts the other (*see figure 5*).

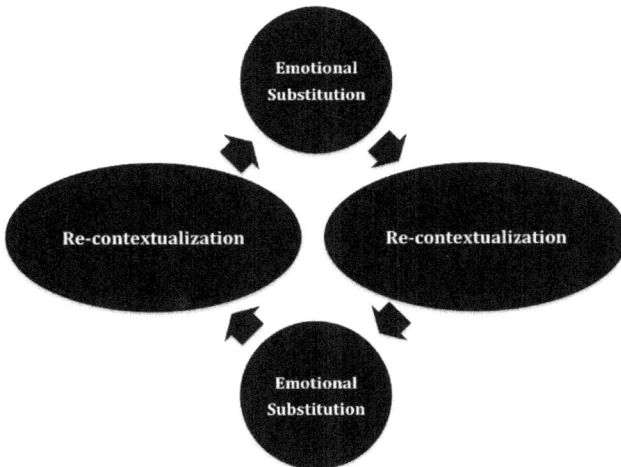

Figure 5 – *Re-contextualization, Emotional Substitution, Re-contextualization Cycle*

We will identify, in this chapter, biblical characters that can help us comprehended more fully the re-contextualization principles involved in extending forgiveness. I believe you will simultaneously appreciate that referencing such characters is more than just another accounting of the stories that you may be familiar with. Maybe, what I am experiencing, as I type this segment, can help make this point.

I am sitting in the back of my residence, and there is a lawn separating the property from a wooded area that has a few ponds situated on it. Can you guess what I am listening to? I have been listening to it for a few days now, since the season began to change, in earnest, from winter to spring. The sound is relatively new to me because I have not been living at this residence for more than a year. Did you guess it? It is the loud chorus of frogs, with notes ranging from high to low in their various croaks.

Still, in the back of my residence, I am also noticing the first of the flowering buds, signaling that spring has arrived. I believe that they are lilies, yellow in color, and I have the delight of experiencing something new – the opening of a flower during the time I spent typing this work.

Why did I relay my experiences with nature? Surely, I have heard and seen frogs and flowers before! However, my experience with them, in the back of my residence, was new and different – they provided fresh offerings. It is hoped that just as I experienced the newness of the croaking frogs and the blooming lilies that we would experience a refreshing newness with regard to extending forgiveness through the perspectives provided by the biblical company of the offended. I also hope that you enjoyed our brief excursion.

Esau

We now continue with the story of Esau, the first in our company of the offended. He found himself within the context of partial family alliances. Esau was loved by his father, Isaac, because he was a hunter and had a taste for game, while his brother, Jacob, was loved by his mother, Rebekah. Such obvious alliances are the breeding ground for potential strife and discord among family members, and the same impacted Isaac's household.

Isaac was ready to bless Esau, his firstborn, because he was advanced in age and did not know the time of his death. Having been asked to prepare a savory meal the way Isaac liked it, Esau anticipated his blessing. But in a treacherous move, Jacob and Rebekah deceived Isaac and the blessing was irrevocably given to Jacob – something that Esau had looked forward to receiving was taken away from him. He suffered a great loss and felt the emotional pain of it: "'Do you have only one blessing, my father? Bless me, me also, O my Father.' So, Esau lifted his voice and wept" (Genesis 27:38).

During this period in history, the bestowal of the blessing was significant. This was especially the case with the posterity of Abraham because he had a covenant relationship with the Creator. Therefore, as the son of Abraham, Isaac's blessing was of great value to Esau. The blessing implied the transfer of great prosperity. This is seen in the blessing that Isaac gave to Jacob that was intended for Esau:

> Now may God give you of the dew of heaven, and of the fatness
> of the earth, and an abundance of grain and new wine; may
> peoples serve you, and nations bow down to you; be master of
> your brothers, and may your mother's sons bow down to you.
> Cursed be those who curse you, and blessed be those who bless
> you (Genesis 27:28-29).

Such a blessing belonged to the firstborn, and Isaac wanted to bestow it on Esau, just as much as Esau desired it. But an offense, through deception, blocked Esau from receiving the blessing and he consoled himself by plotting to kill Jacob after his father's death. What has become interesting in this great cycle of offense, unforgiveness, and offense is the level of respect Esau maintained for his father. Esau did not want to kill his brother while his father was alive. So, in the context of a perverse intention, the killing of a brother, which is not condoned by the Creator, we see a measure of propriety with regard to Isaac. This perspective has certain utility that will be developed later.

Rebekah got wind of Esau's plot and commanded Jacob to leave their home and live with her brother, Laban. Rebekah, with an understanding of the process of forgiveness, told Jacob, "Stay with him a few days, until your brother's fury subsides, until your brother's anger against you subsides and he forgets what you did to him..." (Genesis 27:44-45). Do you see the emotional substitution in Esau's fury and anger subsiding? Yet, of significance is that Esau would eventually forget what was done to him.

Now, we know that forgetting does not mean that Esau would not have any memory of the offense, because the brain "files" our experiences for adaptive purposes. Do you recall "The Miller Effect?" Well, we are on a good foundation if we understand that forgetting, in this context, has to do with Esau, who decides, through emotional substitution, not to pay attention to the offense. In other words, Rebekah had intentions to summon Jacob back home when she perceived that Esau no longer noticed or concerned himself with the offense.

When Jacob returned twenty years later, it was evident that Esau did not notice or pay attention to the offense. Yet, fear gripped Jacob on his journey home because of his imminent encounter with Esau. Jacob learned that Esau was approaching him, accompanied by four hundred men. Jacob's fear drove him to petition the Creator: "Deliver me, I pray, from the hand of my brother, from the hand of Esau; for I fear him, that he will come and attack me and the mothers with the children" (Genesis 32:11).

I indicated earlier that there is the possibility that because of unforgiveness, the offended could cage themselves in psychologically. Still, here we see that the offender can be "caged in" also. Jacob did not have peace of mind because of his offensive behavior towards Esau. Over the years, the guilt of an offense can continue to harm the offender's emotions and functioning if he or she perceives that the offense has not been forgiven.

In the case of Esau, he had torn from around his neck, the yoke of unforgiveness that came through Jacob's offense. By the time they met, the yoke was gone! The anger and the fury had subsided. He did not concern himself with the offense any longer. You may have realized that Scripture does not generally hold Esau in a good moral light, as he despised his birthright, selling it for a single meal. But in his reunion with his brother Jacob, he shines in his nobility by extending forgiveness to him.

It must have been a sight to behold as the offended met the offender: "Then Esau ran to meet him and embraced him, and fell on his neck and kissed him, and they wept" (Genesis 33:4). There was no Esau killing Jacob, for the grudge was gone. Esau extended grace or favor to Jacob, who said, "'No, please, if now I have found favor in your sight, then take my present from my hand, for I see your face as one sees the face of God, and you have received me favorably'" (Genesis 33:10).

The psychological guilt that was manifested in fear weighed heavily upon Jacob, but the fear was lifted. Why? Because he was the recipient of his brother's goodwill, as seen in Esau's kind words and gesture: "'Please let me leave with you some of the people who are with me'" (Genesis 33:15).

The tearing of the yoke of unforgiveness from around Esau's neck was not a facade; it was genuine. This is implied through the continued harmonious relationship that Esau and Jacob shared, post their reunion. There was peace in the relationship. This peace allowed them to work together. "Isaac breathed his last and died and was gathered to his people, an old man of ripe age; and his sons Esau and Jacob buried him" (Genesis 35:29).

Scripture does not provide us with the exact time when Esau removed the yoke of unforgiveness from around his neck. However, we can assume that he was emotionally restless with unforgiveness until that point. It would have been good for us to understand Esau's re-contextualization experience with the offense. Our understanding would include the different perspective(s) acquired that led him to extend grace to his brother. These remain a mystery. Still, it is good to know that he got to that place and has become a good reference point for us in this process of extending forgiveness.

Our foundation of re-contextualization gets on the way with a principle that is gleaned from the life of Esau; it is *the principle of volitional release* (***see figure 6***). This principle focuses on the capacity of the offended. It also makes the distinction between the offended and the offense.

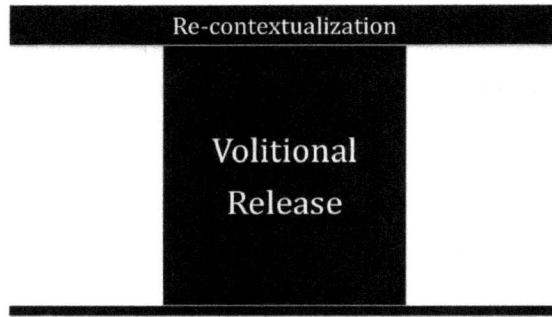

Figure 6 – *A Foundation for Re-contextualization*

Within man, there is a complex set of emotions and cognitive processes that serve his free will or his ability to choose. Our actions are shaped by the way we feel and think. "What is it that I will have for dinner?" you may ask. You decide that you will go out for dinner and so you start to drive to the nearest restaurant. However, midway into your drive, you begin to reason that to eat out will cost thirty dollars. But there is a critical bill that needs to be paid in a few days, and to eat out will make it difficult to do so. Consequently, you scale down a bit. Instead of going to the restaurant, you go to a fast-food establishment and order a chicken sandwich with a side salad.

What just happened? You exercised volition, your free will, and altered your behavior due to your psychological reasoning. It is a part of our human experience, and it is what we do, day in and day out – exercise volition.

Volition, as a resource within us, can also be deployed with regard to an offense. Therefore, we can ask ourselves, "What am I going to do with this offense?" The question implies that the ability of the offended to choose is still intact in an offensive situation. There are options in dealing with the offense, including how it is allowed to shape our emotions and behavior.

As the offender is not the offense, so it is that the offended is not the offense. Making this distinction is essential, so the offended can appreciate that although an offense has occurred, there exists, between them and the offense, a space or separation and a line of demarcation. By making this distinction, the function of volition can be given critical room to operate in such a space, and the confusing, pervasive, and intrusive qualities of an offense can be mitigated. It is in this distinction that the offended finds, amidst the copious potential responses to an offense, the option of volitional release.

Volitional release amplifies the cognitive awareness of the offended and there is the understanding that they could decide how an offense will impact their life. In volitional release, there is also the understanding that those offended have the option of exercising their free will in pardoning the debtor or keeping the offender bound to the debt. They should also know the cost attached to keeping the offender bound to the debt of an offense – there is emotional restlessness!

Awareness of our capacity to exercise volitional release also moves competency to the fore of our understanding of selfhood. Self-competency assures the offended that if they choose to free the offender from the debt, in a volitional release, then they are able to do so successfully.

With volitional release merged with self-competency, one almost gets the feeling that the offended is saying, "I got this," or "I can release my offender from her debt." As you already know, this is not to say that the process of extending forgiveness is an easy one. I am conscious of the fact that some losses are hurtfully painful and that there is a cost attached to extending forgiveness. Just the same, there is a cost attached to unforgiveness. Yet, consistent with our make-up and capacity, we have the viable option of volitional release regarding the debt of our offenders.

Jacob's Joseph

Next, in our company of the offended, is Joseph, the son of Jacob. He too, found himself in an alliance because his father loved him more than all of his brothers. Jacob demonstrated his love for Joseph when he made him a coat of many colors. Jacob's partial love towards Joseph contributed to the intense hatred that his brothers had towards him. It was indicated earlier, that when there are family alliances, there is potential for relationship failure among family members. We see this in Jacob's household, as we saw it in Isaac's.

Additionally, Joseph's reporting on his brothers' improper behavior to their father, along with the dreams that he had, which positioned him to a place of honor above, not only his brothers, but also his father and mother, kept him as the object of his brothers' bitter hatred.

One day Jacob sent Joseph to check on the affairs of his brothers, who were taking care of their sheep away from their home. Seeing Joseph from a distance, and filled with their hatred for him, they conspired to kill him. However, a caravan of traders traveling towards Egypt provided for an alternative means of getting rid of him, so his brothers sold him into slavery.

In Egypt, he thrived because of the Creator's hand on his life. Joseph also encountered adversity and was thrown into prison due to false accusations from a lust-crazed woman.

So, Joseph suffered the loss of his home, family relations, and freedom through the offense of his brothers. For many years, he had no contact with his father, younger brother, sister, or even his hateful brothers. Eventually, his circumstances changed. From prison, he was elevated to the second place of authority over the land of Egypt because, through the power of the Creator, he was able to interpret the dreams of Pharaoh, ruler of Egypt.

Pharaoh's dreams revealed that a seven-year period of abundance was to be followed by another seven-year period, but this time, of famine. Through Joseph's wisdom and policy directives, during the years of abundance, sufficient grain was stored up in Egypt to take care of the food needs of not only the people of Egypt, but also the people of the surrounding regions, which included Jacob's family.

Consequently, Joseph's brothers were sent to Egypt to buy grain to sustain their families. While in Egypt, they encountered Joseph, and although they did not recognize him, he recognized them. It is here that the story becomes more pertinent to our concern. In their initial encounter, Joseph did not reveal himself to his brothers, but rather tested them by accusing them of being spies who entered the land of Egypt to identify its vulnerable or undefended parts. I believe the test was orchestrated by Joseph to gather information about the family he had lost contact with for many years. In addition, he wanted to find out what was in his brothers' hearts after many years of separation.

Scripture supports, however, that while in a position of power that afforded him the opportunity to be vindictive, he instead, showed his brothers kindness when they were sent away to return home: "Then Joseph gave orders to fill their bags with grain and to restore every man's money in his sack, and to give them provisions for the journey. And thus it was done for them" (Genesis 42:25).

Although Scripture does not say outright that Joseph extended forgiveness to his brothers for the wrong they perpetrated against him, it is evident or implied that he did. Joseph's kind dealings with his brothers indicated that he had forgiven them and that he no longer paid attention to the offenses they perpetrated against him.

Upon the brothers' return to Egypt, Joseph revealed himself to them and, once again, gave indication that he had released them from the debt that they had incurred when they offended him: "He kissed all his brothers and wept on them, and afterward his brothers talked with him" (Genesis 45:15).

Joseph's forgiveness was thoroughly extended to his brothers. Following the death of Jacob, some seventeen years after the family's reunion with Joseph, the brothers feared for their lives. They reasoned that Joseph might still bear a grudge and would take vengeance upon them, now that their father was dead. Here, we are reminded of the psychological encaging and emotional unrest that offenders also experience.

However, the relationally affirming words of Joseph, in his response to their fears, revealed the completeness of his forgiveness:

> But Joseph said to them, 'Do not be afraid, for am I in God's place? As for you, you meant evil against me, but God meant it for good in order to bring about this present result, to preserve many people alive. So therefore, do not be afraid: I will provide for you and your little ones.' So, he comforted them and spoke kindly to them (Genesis 50:19-21).

Joseph's response to his brothers' fears is multilayered in what it offers. First, by asking, "…am I in God's place?" Joseph recognized that

79

there is another, the Creator, who sees injustice, and He has His way of dealing with it. Joseph respected that! Second, the offense perpetrated by the brothers, although not excusable, had a different purpose in Joseph's life, as the Creator handled it. Through His providential working or actions in their affairs, as human beings, when the brothers meant the offense for evil, the Creator meant it for good. Third, the response, underscored Joseph's release of his brothers from their debt, as he graciously affirmed that he would continue to do what he was already doing for them, that is, provide for them.

Forgiving his brothers also translated into a scene where he comforted and spoke kindly to them. It stands to reason then that, in extending forgiveness, those forgiven should, where possible, experience behavior(s) from the offended that is in harmony with the act of forgiveness. Joseph's brothers would have probably been confused and would have had reason to fear if he had said, "I forgive you," but spoke in a vitriolic way and/or acted abusively towards them.

The providential working of the Creator, in the life of Joseph, is further seen when he revealed himself to his brothers in Egypt:

> Now do not be grieved or angry with yourselves, because you sold me here, for God sent me before you to preserve life. For the famine has been in the land these two years, and there are still five years in which there will be neither plowing nor harvesting. God sent me before you to preserve for you a remnant in the earth, and keep you alive by a great deliverance" (Genesis 45:5-7).

So, from Joseph's perspective, his brothers sold him into Egyptian slavery, but as the caravan carrying him was moving towards Egypt, it was the Creator that was sending him with a purpose to that country – to work deliverance for the peoples of that region and beyond. It is this perspective of Joseph that provides us with our next principle that aids in giving new meaning to the offense, and therefore, is a part of our re-contextualization foundation, specifically, *the principle of the broadened view* (*see figure 7*).

This principle encourages the offended to lift their head and courageously look beyond, around, to the left and to right of the offense.

Is there something that can be seen in the context of the offense that may be considered as working for you, the offended? Is there a benefit for others through the offense? Can you see it?

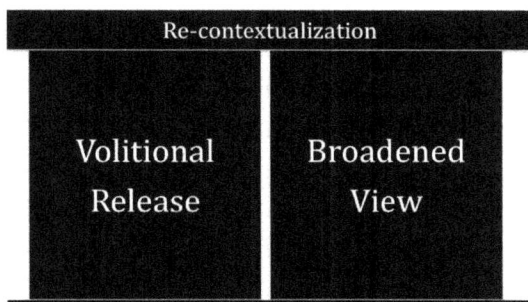

Figure 7 – *A Foundation for Re-contextualization*

The offense entered "the room" of your life, but what else came along with it? Was it opportunity? Consider the case of the individual who was unjustly terminated from her place of employment. She needed to maintain an income, so she started a small business that became very profitable. To the extent that, although the offense through her former employment, at that time, seemed significant, it no longer was, given her successful outcome. And given the chance, she would probably kiss her former boss for firing her because it worked out for her good, as well as for those who patronize her business.

Was it an occasion for pause in your marriage plans when your fiancé called you "Stupid?" All you did was accidentally roll over some of his flowering plants with your vehicle while visiting! The offense provided you with the opportunity to really consider the qualities of the person that you intended to marry and ask the salient questions: "Do I want to marry someone who will break me down with his words?" or "Do I want to marry someone who will be encouraging and who will build me up with his words?"

In Joseph's case, he understood that the Creator worked through the offense of his brothers. Consider the offense you may have suffered at the hands of someone, do you see the Creator advantageously adding to or taking away from your life? Joseph was able to forget about the days of affliction (he paid no attention to them) because of the additions to his life, post the wrong done to him. With regard to his sons, who were born to him in Egypt, "'Joseph named the firstborn Manasseh, 'For,' he said, 'God has made me forget all my trouble and all my father's household.' He named the second Ephraim, 'For,' he said, 'God has made me fruitful in the land of my affliction'" (Genesis 41:51-52).

To the one accustomed to being abused by her husband: Since his arrest for physically abusing you, do you see yourself being liberated, no longer fearful or encaged so that you are able to be yourself? Your husband can now get the professional help that he needs to deal with his anger problem. His rehabilitation may lead to the marriage becoming whole again and more of a blessing to both of you.

The broadened view also provides for self-evaluation and the possible consequent relational improvement of the offended. The offender is responsible for their actions, but it may be that the offended behavior contributed to the offensive experience. Do you remember our offense, unforgiveness, offense cycle? If it is understood that I, as the offended, could have said or done something differently, in hindsight, that might have impacted positively how things turned out in an offensive situation, then that is something that I can appreciate. It would help me to adjust my behavior in the future, as I seek to become more adept in my interpersonal and relational skills and more intentional with regard to not offending others.

Mary's Joseph

The next person, who can be found in the company of the offended, is arguably Joseph, the fiancé and later husband of Mary, who was the mother of Jesus, the Creator's Son. I say arguably because not much is provided in Scripture about the life of Joseph prior to or post the birth of Jesus. Therefore, his life is opened for much conjecture or speculation. I will do a little conjecturing that should be in line or in tune with what is implied from the Scriptures that reveal something regarding Joseph. Our concern is with Joseph, who was engaged to the virgin, Mary.

Mary received a celestial visitor, in the angel Gabriel, who informed her that she was highly favored by the Creator and that she would conceive and bear a Son who was to be called Jesus. The process was to be a miraculous one brought about by the Holy Spirit of the Creator. It was to be an extraordinary conceptual process that deviated from the natural conjugal behavior involving a man and a woman.

Mary's favor before the Creator was understandable since she was willing to submit to His bidding for her life: "And Mary said, 'Behold, the bondslave of the Lord; may it be done to me according to your word.' And the angel departed from her" (Luke 1:38).

What is implied from this account is that this news of the Creator's intentions and work towards Mary did not "sit" too well with Joseph, because he was planning to break off their engagement:

> Now the birth of Jesus Christ was as follows: when His mother Mary had been betrothed [*engaged*] to Joseph, before they came together she was found to be with child by the Holy Spirit. And Joseph her husband, being a righteous man and not wanting to disgrace her, planned to send her away secretly (Matthew 1:18-19).

There is also implication that Joseph was offended and hurt by the prospect of being engaged to a woman who was supposed to be a virgin, but now was with child. In Joseph's heart, perhaps, there was some suspicion regarding Mary's fidelity. According to the natural order of things C follows A+B; Joseph knew that a child on the way was the result of the conjugal behavior of a man and a woman. Who would not think this way? Therefore, he needed help to understand that what Mary was experiencing was a supernatural, or out of the natural, event.

So, the Creator provided the help that Joseph needed, which was also a supernatural occurrence for an angel appeared to him in a dream to allay his suspicion or apprehension, and to thwart his separation plans towards Mary:

> But when he had considered this, behold, an angel of the Lord appeared to him in a dream, saying, 'Joseph, son of David, do not be afraid to take Mary as your wife; for the child who has been conceived in her is of the Holy Spirit. She will bear a Son; and you shall call His name Jesus, for He will save His people from their sins (Matthew 1:20-21).

A Savior was on the way and Joseph accepted his part in the process; he took Mary to be his wife and subsequently functioned as a husband towards her. However, our interest is in Joseph's stance while he was under the possible notion that some mortal man made a breach into his personal space, and caused him loss by violating his treasure, in the virgin, Mary. It is in this that we find another principle for our re-contextualization foundation. Joseph's stance of not wanting to disgrace Mary publicly, because of the perceived offense, was based on his character. He was a righteous man!

He wanted to respond in a way that was unconventional in his culture; he wanted to shield Mary from the disgrace that accompanied those who acted treacherously and contradicted their moral character and obligations. We know that Mary was not behaving treacherously for her condition was extraordinarily linked to the Creator's plan for her life and did not involve any moral breach.

However, the prospect that someone acted unfaithfully was punishable by public denouncement and even death in Joseph's culture. Yet, Joseph, although he conceived a plan to separate himself from Mary, wanted to do so while showing her kindness – he planned a secret severance. Our foundation principle therefore is *the principle of integrity of character* (**see figure 8**).

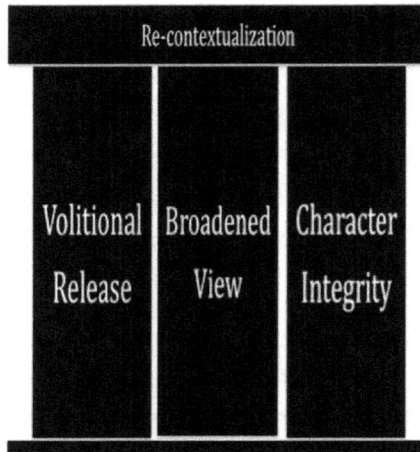

Figure 8 – *A Foundation for Re-contextualization*

This principle helps the offended realize that they can act unconventionally, in response to an offense – that the offender can be treated differently than they might deserve. But this difference in response, while it impacts the offender, stems from the character or disposition of the offended. Because of who you are (law-abiding, lover of people, productive, belonging to the Creator, adherent to morality, "bestower" of that which is good, interested in the wellbeing of others, and a builder) the response to the offense is not one that is in kind. So, the unkind, selfish, offensive act can be met with kindness and goodness, which come out of the core or inner structures of who you are.

Since you are used to doing good and being kind to others, these qualities that define you can continue beyond the offense. Scripture points those of us who belong to the Creator in this direction:

> But if your enemy is hungry, feed him, and if he is thirsty, give him a drink: for in so doing you will heap burning coals on his head. Do not be overcome by evil, but overcome evil with good (Romans 12:20-21).

You are known to act in a certain kind and gentle way, so who you are, already positions you to give a drink of water to the offender, where possible; it is a natural occurrence for you in this respect. Therefore, because of your tendency to be kind, extending forgiveness will only reflect more of your character; you will be functioning out of it!

In a poultry processing plant, a quality control officer became the object of the venomous language of a maintenance worker; perhaps, new quality control measures were not being happily received. One day, there was a major breakdown in the plant's processing equipment and everything came to a standstill. The maintenance worker was now in the spotlight, as he tried to remedy the situation; all eyes were on him.

The quality control officer was oblivious to what had happened in the plant because he was in a different area of the facility. So, when he entered the processing area and drew near to where the problem and efforts to remedy it were, he was met with an intense, loud, reverberating, "Get him from…(expletive)…around me. I don't want him around me!" from the maintenance worker. All who were assembled there, around the center of the problem, heard him. Having a more senior position in the plant than the maintenance worker, the quality control officer determined that enough was enough and took him to the office of the personnel manager.

At the meeting, the quality control officer could have insisted that a severe form of disciplinary action be taken against the maintenance worker, but he told the personnel manager that he did not want him to lose his job, that all he wanted was a change in his attitude and the way he was being spoken to by the maintenance worker. The request was acceptable to all, and the maintenance worker left the office of the personnel manager smiling.

That office experience was the turning point in the relationship between the quality control officer and the maintenance worker; their relationship improved, significantly. It revealed kindness for insults, love for hate, and goodwill for ill will. It revealed actions that were consistent with the character of the quality control officer, which was one that had the best interests of others at heart.

Moreover, it proves that an offense need not displace benevolent acts, even when we face malevolent ones.

Jesus

I indicated above that a Savior was on the way, in the supernatural gestation experience of Mary. He was embodied in the historical Jesus of Nazareth, who traveled the territory of Palestine some two millennia ago. The process of His salvation was also unconventional. It did not involve the toppling of an earthly regime by another, the invading of one country with the military might of another, or the banding together of the forces of resistance determined to overthrow the government in their country.

Rather, His salvation was worked through an instrument of death – a cross, refined by the Roman authorities to deliver an effective and torturous death to criminals. It served as a reminder to others of what could be done to them, if their actions were not in keeping with society's orderly norms.

It is this Jesus that helps to round out our company of the offended as we build or set our re-contextualization foundation. His words, while on His cross and near death, are pertinent to our concern: "But Jesus was saying, 'Father, forgive them; for they do not know what they are doing.' And they cast lots, dividing up His garments among themselves" (Luke 23:34).

The request that the Father forgive those who contributed to His being on the cross had to be actualized in the lives of those whom Jesus prayed for on that fateful day, but the prayer revealed His predisposition; which was one that was inclined to extend forgiveness to those who offended Him. In this vein, He too functioned out of the integrity of His character. And because of it, He did not respond in kind to those who participated in nailing Him to His cross.

However, to have a fuller appreciation of this request of Jesus, that is, that the Father forgive them, it is good for us to take a glimpse at what preceded it. One of his close followers, Judas Iscariot, betrayed Him for thirty pieces of silver, despite receiving 'good' from His lips and hands, and seeing the extraordinary way the Creator worked through His life. This follower saw extraordinary miracles, including the healing of all manner of diseases and Jesus walking on water, but a betrayal was given in exchange for good.

The "them," that Jesus asked His Father to forgive also included His own people who were the objects of wonderful teachings and goodness from His miraculous hands; particularly, the leaders of the people who envied His favorable status and popularity during His work on earth. Despite the good they received, on the morning of his crucifixion, the people were persuaded to say, "'Crucify, crucify Him'" (Luke 23:21), even though there was no just cause to do so, and when provided with an opportunity to aid in His release, they repaid Him evil for good.

Indeed, the offense perpetrated against Jesus was egregious! For there was no just cause for Him to have died the kind of death that He died, which was suited for the vilest of criminals. But through the ill motives of conspirators, in the leaders of His people, false accusations were fabricated against Him. And because of a weak and selfishly ambitious Roman governor, who was vested with the instrument of death, and who knew that Jesus had not done anything deserving of it, the will of the people was allowed to prevail – Jesus was crucified. However, this miscarriage of justice, as evidenced in Jesus' crucifixion, was not done in a vacuum. The Creator was aware of it, for a prophetic word foretold it: "In his humiliation justice was denied him…" (Acts 8:33, New Revised Standard Version - NRSV).

Our picture of the offense and its accompanying injustice will not be complete if some of the events of the actual crucifixion of Jesus are left out. Offense came to Jesus when His clothing was removed, and nails were driven through His hands and feet, which held His body to the cross. Subsequently, He was lifted on the cross to be exposed to the elements, and public ridicule. The offense of the cross came after a crown of thorns was plaited, placed, and pressed down on His head. Also, it came after a severe beating that underscored the governor's attempt to dissuade the people from desiring His death. And so, the cross, perpetuated the injuries of Jesus' offense, and then, it took it to another level – it caused His agonizing death.

So, "Father forgive them, for they do not know what they are doing," are words that were spoken as a result of an exemplary model of emotional substitution. It included substituting goodwill for ill will, love for hatred, and mercy for unkindness. If at this point you are looking at this picture and acknowledging that such a disposition should be yours, it would be understandable if you say, "What a challenging task, I need help!" Fortunately, the Creator provides help through His Holy Spirit for those who submit to His will.

It is in Jesus' prayer on the cross, that we find the final principle for our re-contextualization foundation, particularly in these words, "… for they do not know what they are doing." It is called *the principle of deficiency* (**see figure 9**). The principle of deficiency has implications for the offended, as well as the offender. We know that lack or the thing that is missing can be found in all concerned with an offense, but our emphasis, at this juncture, is on the lack or deficiency that is with the offender.

This principle does not excuse the offense or the offender with their concomitant deficiency; rather, it asks the offended to acknowledge it. In other words, some underlying cause or the absence of something can be identified in an offender's life that led to the offense. Such deficiencies could include, belief structures devoid of moral imprints; a worldview that has at its center *the self* with very little, if any, consideration for others; emotional failures due to impaired attachment patterns in an individual's early development; inappropriate dependency, which reflects the absence of a functional relational autonomy; and, intrusion tendencies that suggests that someone has not learned to respect the relational and emotional boundaries of others. All of these become the breeding ground for an offense. They all imply that something is lacking in the offender.

Jesus implied that those who contributed to His crucifixion operated without knowledge; they were ignorant of something. The full picture was not theirs, particularly, the crowds who were swayed by the envious religious leaders of His day. They were blinded and cut off from critical understanding and, in oblivion, worked a most unfortunate offense against an innocent Man.

How does understanding and acknowledgment of the offender's deficiency fit within the framework of the re-contextualization of an offense and thereby aid the offended in the processes of extending forgiveness through empathy? The offense is not perceived as an isolated event but as having impoverished antecedents. Consequently, the offended could say, "Had this been in place, she might have acted differently," or "I am not excusing his actions, but what he said gives me reason to question the events of his background."

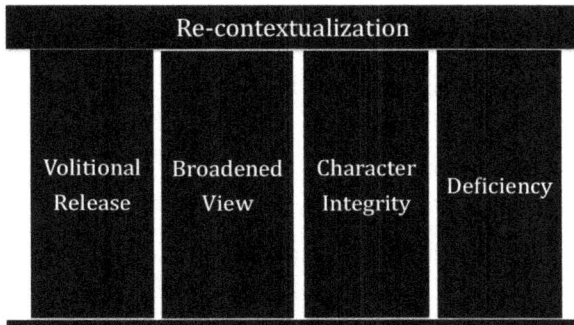

Re-contextualization			
Volitional Release	Broadened View	Character Integrity	Deficiency

Figure 9 – *A Foundation for Re-contextualization*

89

It is appropriate here to point out that while some individuals may be cold and uncaring when they offend others, some do not want to offend. They do not see themselves in a good place if they were to offend others, and they do not want to be there. However, they find it difficult to not offend, even when they do not want to. The habitual patterns have set in, so extricating themselves from the tendency to offend is like trying to remove a piece of eggshell from the egg white in a bowl, while preparing to make some scrambled eggs.

The more you try to pull up the piece of shell with your finger (that is what I use), the more the white pulls it back down. Eventually, the "chef" removes the piece of shell because it is not acceptable to have a shell crunch with scrambled eggs.

As the removal of the eggshell could be very challenging, it can be a great hurdle for some offenders to break the difficult offending habit even though they realize that the habit is unacceptable, both for them and others. Fortunately, there is therapy to help extricate an individual from those offending habits that diminish human dignity and functionality.

Also, from a more comprehensive vantage point, the Creator offers help that addresses offending behaviors through the invitation His Son (Jesus, the Christ) extends to humanity:

> Come to Me, all who are weary and heavy-laden, and I will give you rest. Take My yoke upon you and learn from Me, for I am gentle and humble in heart, and you will find rest for your souls. For My yoke is easy and My burden is light (Matthew 11:28-30).

With all sensitivity to the gravity of certain offenses, we have formed our re-contextualization foundation. In doing so, it is hoped that the offended can see it as a resource to gain a new perspective on a particular offense and/or the offender. Such a perspective can lead to the action of emotional substitution, which is a critical consideration when one decides to extend forgiveness.

Our foundation is formed by the principles of volitional release, broadened view, integrity of character, and deficiency. However, it is not an exhaustive list of principles. One can see these standards as initial steps in the right direction towards re-contextualization and emotional substitution. As we continue our journey together, you will easily identify another principle that can be added to this foundation. And now, we will take a closer look at what is involved when the Creator extends forgiveness.

For further deliberation…

1. What might we learn from the offender's tendency to adhere to some good?

2. Volition, competency, and choice can all work together to give the offended a new perspective of the offense and offender. Do you agree? Why or why not?

3. What is the cost of forgiveness against that of unforgiveness?

4. Courage is needed to look beyond and see the good that an offense may bring to the offended. How might courage benefit the offended in this challenging time of their life?

5. How important is it for the offended to acknowledge their role that may have contributed to the offense?

I Forgive

Chapter Five

When the Creator Forgives…

"I know that God would want me to forgive him."
— ***Karen Woodside***

The Creator could easily be included in our company of the offended! Really? Yes, He is right there among them. However, He requires special consideration because of all that He means to us as human beings. You see, while He extends forgiveness to His offenders, He also functions as our Lawgiver, Judge, and the One that we must give an account to in the day He has set for judging us all. No, we do not just live this life and, in it, do what we feel like doing, or say what we want to say, or even think what we want to think without having to give an account to Him, our Creator.

As we will see, the various functions of the Creator have a direct impact on the nature of the forgiveness that He extends to us. However, as we bring the Creator's forgiveness a little closer into view, it is hoped that we will find utility in it to help us in this process of extending forgiveness. As the Creator is a fitting example for other areas of our mutual moral "oughtness," so He is when it comes to extending forgiveness. Consequently, we can go to Him for a refined and proper perspective on it.

We have already seen that the Creator is, and wants to become, intimate with us as human beings. We have also seen that He is also offended when we violate His code of conduct or laws for our lives. A divine code for human behavior is critically linked to His prerogative as Creator. Therefore, having been enjoined to it, we can embrace the view that the thing created does not say to the Creator, "I don't like the way you made me," or "I don't like what you require of me." The semblance of this divine code is pervasively seen throughout our world, in what I have been referring to as our mutual moral "oughtness."

However, the Creator has not left it to chance with regard to us knowing His code for our lives. Today, the Creator reveals His will for our lives through His Son, Christ Jesus:

> God, after He spoke long ago to the fathers in the prophets in many portions and in many ways, in these last days has spoken to us in His Son, whom He appointed heir of all things, through whom also He made the world (Hebrews 1:1-2).

Again, we find our attention being directed to the Son: "'...This is My beloved Son, with whom I am well-pleased; listen to Him'" (Matthew 17:5)!

So, we are not left up to our own devices when it comes to morality and what it takes to please the Creator. Ultimately, we are answerable to the Creator's laws through His Son. This is one of the reasons why the Creator must be treated differently from us in this concern we have regarding extending forgiveness. We do not have the prerogative to extend the universal laws for all of humankind, but the Creator does, and He has exercised such a prerogative.

Therefore, the Creator sits high as Lawgiver, today, through His Son, but He also sits high as Judge. And, have you guessed it yet? He will judge the world through His Son:

> Therefore, having overlooked the times of ignorance, God is now declaring to men that all people everywhere should repent, because He has fixed a day in which He will judge the world in righteousness through a Man whom He has appointed, having furnished proof to all men by raising Him from the dead (Acts 17:30-31).

This world needs the highest Supreme Court; and we have it in the Creator's court, which is to come. The injustice that went undetected and not dealt with by limited human sight and judiciary will not escape the judgment of the highest court. More than this, every thought, word, and deed will be factored into this comprehensive judgment to come:

For we must all appear before the judgment seat of Christ, so that each one may be recompensed for his deeds in the body, according to what he has done whether good or bad (2 Corinthians 5:10).

When I think about the hardships computer and Internet fraudsters place on the unsuspecting, particularly the elderly and the ignorant, through their fake websites that rob them of their hard-earned income, I also think that they will not escape the highest court given their breach in our mutual moral "oughtness." Neither you, nor I, have the power, right, capacity, or insight to become the lawgiver and judge for humankind, but the Creator does.

Our human behavior, which can be so immoral at times, constrains Him to act as our Judge. He is the Lawgiver and out of His just character He must deal with the wrong that deviates from His ideal for humanity:

Then the Lord passed by in front of him [*Moses*] and proclaimed, 'The Lord, the Lord God, compassionate and gracious, slow to anger, and abounding in lovingkindness and truth: who keeps lovingkindness for thousands, who forgives iniquity, transgression and sin; yet He will by no means leave the guilty unpunished, visiting the iniquity of fathers on the children and on the grandchildren to the third and fourth generation (Exodus 34:6-7).

The latter portion of this reference may cause some consternation, but do not worry about it. The Creator's visitation is not arbitrary so we can rest assured that His behavior is right in human affairs for righteousness and justice are the foundation of His throne. Else, how will He be a just and righteous judge when we stand before Him in the day of accounting?

So, the offenses, that breach the Creator's code for human behavior, that is, in iniquity (wickedness), transgression (violation of the law), and sin (an immoral act) can be forgiven. The Creator can release the offender from the debt that they incurred when they violated His laws for human behavior.

Therefore, we have the Creator as Judge, and in this role, He functions above human behavior. His judgment will take into consideration what we have done with our capacity to forgive. For instance, with regard to the Creator's people, when they fail to forgive their fellow human beings of their offenses, this will result in their offenses not being forgiven by the Creator.

We also see the Creator participating in the phenomenon of extending forgiveness, as He releases His human offenders from their debt. However, such release is conditional. In this, we see a clear distinction with regard to extending forgiveness. For us it is an imperative, particularly, if we want to please Him, but for the Creator it is conditional!

This conditional release is linked to: 1) the Creator's prerogative over His creation – He has the right to regulate the release and retention of human debt; 2) His function as Judge of the world – He determines what to do with those whose debt have been retained or removed; and, 3) our volition or free will as human beings – we decide if we are going to embrace the conditions attached to the Creator's release of our debts.

It might as well be brought into the open – the Creator has invested heavily in us as human beings and He wants to be given His due; it is only right that our Maker be respected, obeyed, and loved. Today, love for the Creator is hinged on each of us keeping His commandments that are found under the New Covenant or agreement between Him and His people. This New Covenant was initiated through the death of His Son, Christ Jesus; it is comprised of laws that we can read about in the New Testament section of the Bible.

When man chooses to disobey His Creator, he decides to follow a path that is not pleasing before Him. It is a path that will cause man to negatively experience the predetermined judgment to come. Therefore, to try and put it succinctly: The Judge of the whole world can release us from the debt(s) of our offense(s), through the exercise of our free will, as we obey His conditional terms.

The good news is that although man has offended his Creator, he can be released from his debt, no matter the nature, degree, and duration of the offense. Is not that good news? Release is possible because of the lovingkindness and grace of the Creator, manifested in the cross of His Son.

It has already been revealed that Jesus died unjustly, but that is not the full extent of the account. While Jesus, the Son of God, was being put to death, the Creator, through His providential working, was also providing for Himself a fitting vicarious sacrifice that enables Him to free or release us (humanity) from the debt of our offense. "Why was such a sacrifice needed?" you may ask. Because it fits the bill!

We became defiled in our spirits when we violated the Creator's law and found ourselves, spiritually, in a hostile and helpless place before Him. Consequently, we needed someone to help us, but that someone had to be blameless. Certainly, we can understand this, can't we? Why look for help from someone that is equally in a helpless state? This would have been the case if we had sought, in humanity, the spiritual help we needed; such help could not be found among us humans.

It took the Creator Himself to divest a part of Himself and come to earth, in His Son, so that the fitting help could be provided for all humanity:

> Have this attitude in yourselves which was also in Christ Jesus, who, although He existed in the form of God, did not regard equality with God a thing to be grasped, but emptied Himself, taking the form of a bond-servant, and being made in the likeness of men. Being found in appearance as a man, He humbled Himself by becoming obedient to the point of death, even death on a cross (Philippians 2:5-8).

Therefore, this Jesus that was unjustly put to death was actually the Creator/God Himself, Who was blameless and willing to provide the help we needed as human beings. "In which way?" you may ask. The death of Jesus was a vicarious or "substitutionary" death. He died for those who have offended God so that they could be brought into a harmonious relationship with Him:

> "For Christ also died for sins once for all, the just for the unjust, so that He might bring us to God, having been put to death in the flesh, but made alive in the spirit…"(1 Peter 3:18).

Still, there is more to the cross of Jesus than a sophisticated means of execution. Through it, the Creator provided a suitable sacrifice for Himself that allowed Him to punish sin: "...and He [*Jesus*] Himself bore our sins in His body on the cross, so that we might die to sin and live to righteousness; for by His wounds you were healed" (1 Peter 2:24). While at the same time He procured the basis for Him to mete out mercy (kindness for injury) towards us for the Just (Jesus) died for the unjust (us offenders).

The Creator, through the cross and blood of Christ Jesus, is able to deal with the penalty of sin (offenses), "For the wages of sin is death, but the free gift of God is eternal life in Christ Jesus our Lord" (Romans 6:23). Additionally, it is because of the death of Christ, man has an opportunity to be reconciled to his Creator.

Therefore, the cross of Christ Jesus, the Son of God, holds tremendous blessings for human beings, even though we have offended Him. However, as indicated earlier, such blessings are conditional. The conditional receipt of the Creator releasing us from the debt of our offense(s) can be understood in the requirement of obedience: "Although He [*Jesus*] was a Son, He learned obedience from the things which He suffered. And having been made perfect, He became to all those who obey Him the source of eternal salvation" (Hebrews 5:8-9). Consequently, it is those who would obey the Son that would experience release from their debt, with eternal implications.

Perhaps, this crude analogy would bring greater clarity. You are in a state of need; the mortgage payment is due; other bills are piling up; and, there is no money to buy food. Just as you are sitting in your house contemplating your immense financial struggle, there is a knock at your door. As you open the door, there standing before you, is a bank representative. He first apologizes for his tardiness in getting to you, but he proceeds to inform you that a close relative passed on and left you a million dollars.

The news causes your emotions to shift from sadness to joy. You start to verbalize your plans for the million dollars. "I am going to buy that apartment complex," you may say. However, the bank representative further informs you that in order for you to receive one dollar from the inheritance you have to go into the bank and fill out some procedural forms. Question: Will you benefit from the million dollars procured for you if you do not go to the bank and fill out the forms?

If you exclaimed, "No!" then you are quite right. Well, just as it is important for you to go to the bank and fill out the forms and then experience the inheritance your relative left for you, so it is that we must obey the Creator in order to experience the invaluable blessings that He has procured for humanity through the death of His Son. No obedience, no partaking! And so, we have the conditional considerations that need to be taken into account, today, if we are to experience forgiveness or secure release from our offensive debt before the Creator.

Conditional Release

As you understand the conditional nature of the forgiveness the Creator extends to us as debtors, you may be asking, "What must we do?" The answer is not, "Nothing!" To be sure, there is nothing that we can do in and of ourselves to remedy our spiritual deficit before the Creator – help was graciously provided for us through the death of the Creator's Son. However, there is something we must do – we must follow the Creator's instructions or will in order to receive the spiritual blessings He extends to us.

Forgiveness from the Creator is extended towards two groups of people in the human experience. The first group consists of those who are not His people, spiritually. They are characterized as belonging to the world or that part of humankind that is under the control or influence of the Creator's enemy, the devil.

Individuals can know if they are a part of this realm by their behavior, which is marked by unrestrained lust and pride that violate the Creator's code for human behavior:

> For all that is in the world, the lust of the flesh and the lust of the eyes and the boastful pride of life, is not from the Father, but is from the world. The world is passing away, and also its lusts; but the one who does the will of God lives forever (1 John 2:16-17).

We also see from the above Scripture text that an individual must do the will of the Creator; therefore, through obedience an individual has the assurance that they have been separated from the realm of the devil and made to be a constituent of the Creator's people or family.

When individuals in the realm or domain of the devil hear the good news about what the Creator has done (in His gracious offerings, procurement of the debt payment, and desire to release them from debt) through His Son Jesus and they believe it, then they are headed in the right direction towards freedom from the debt of their offense(s).

Additionally, they need to repent of any behavior displeasing to the Creator. Repentance has to do with a change of mind with regard to wicked behavior. It involves a turning away from sins (offenses) and a turning to the Creator in order to conform to His will.

For those in the world who desire the Creator's release, they must also acknowledge that Jesus is Lord. If Jesus' Lordship is going to be effective in an individual's life, then it is critical that such a person do what He says. Jesus, Himself said, "Why do you call Me, 'Lord, Lord,' and do not do what I say" (Luke 6:46)?

Before individuals are released or delivered from the debt of their offense, they must be baptized (immersed) in water for the forgiveness of their sins (offenses). Jesus' order to His disciples' underscores this:

> And He said to them, 'Go into all the world and preach the gospel to all creation, He who has believed, and has been baptized shall be saved; but he who has disbelieved shall be condemned (Mark 16:15-16).

The words of one of Jesus' disciples, Peter, after he had proclaimed the message of the gospel, also echoes the instructions of Jesus for the Creator's debtors:

> Now when they heard this, they were pierced to the heart, and said to Peter and the rest of the apostles, 'Brethren, what shall we do?' Peter said to them, 'Repent, and each of you be baptized in the name of Jesus Christ for the forgiveness of your sins; and you will receive the gift of the Holy Spirit' (Acts 2:37-38).

When the Holy Spirit (God's Spirit) is given, Who is the means by which the Creator and His Son make their abode with us today, individuals have the assurance that they: 1) belong to the Creator (Romans 8:9); 2) have access to the spiritual help needed in their walk with the Creator (Romans 8:26); and, 3) have the confidence that they would further be blessed with His promises (Ephesians 1:13-14). The Holy Spirit (God/The Creator), in union with the compliant individual accomplishes much, but note when He comes and abides in a person's spirit – through water baptism, according to Acts 2:38.

And so, we have the Creator's will or requirements for the forgiveness of debt (belief, repentance, admittance of the Lordship of Jesus, and water baptism) for the offenders in the world. "Why water baptism?" one may ask. The Creator, in His wisdom, does an interesting work for the repentant believer through water baptism.

Through this physical act of obedience, the Creator spiritually unites us with His Son's death, burial, and resurrection. In union with the Son's death, our old sin (offense) defiled person or self is put to death. In union with the Son's burial, His blood removes our sins (offenses). And in union with the Son's resurrection, compliant individuals rise to walk in newness of life; they have been born again or made alive in their spirits, having had the stain of sin (offense) removed; and, they are no longer situated in spiritual death.

As noted earlier, release from the debt in offenses takes place at the point of water baptism because that is the point where the Creator applies the merits of Jesus' death on the cross to an individual's life. Jesus' death on the cross is, therefore, a procured ransom payment that allows the Creator to release His offenders from their debt, when they submit to His will.

The apostle Paul reminded the Creator's people of the process in which they were made spiritually alive. He explained to them that the Creator:

> ...made you alive together with Him [*Jesus*], having forgiven us all our transgressions, having canceled out the certificate of debt consisting of decrees against us, which was hostile to us;

and He has taken it out the way; having nailed it to the cross (Colossians 2:13-14).

For them, the cancellation of debt took place when they were baptized (Colossians 2:11-12)! Therefore, it is through water baptism that a believer of the gospel of Christ Jesus experiences the spiritual blessings His cross affords.

In another passage that explains how through baptism an individual unites with Jesus' death (Romans 6:4), Paul, in no uncertain terms, revealed that an individual is freed from sin (offense) when they die spiritually: "For he who has died is freed from sin" (Romans 6:7). Therefore, in order for a person to be freed (released) from sin (offense) today, he or she has to die spiritually with Jesus, and this takes place through water baptism. Much more can be said, but I believe you get the picture.

Of course, the individual who has been made alive, through the release of debt by the gracious offering of the Creator, must remain on the side of life and faithfully adhere to the will of the One who made this release possible. If, as a believer in the good news concerning the Creator's Son, you have not been baptized in water in order to be released from the debt of your sins (offenses), let me encourage you to embrace the Creator's gracious offering and do so!

The second group of offenders consists of those who have been released from their offenses but offend again. I am talking about those that have already been baptized in water and separated from the world and, therefore, constitute the people that belong to the Creator (Matthew 1:21). If they sin again or offend the Creator once more, there are certain instructions for them to follow, so that they could continue to be connected to the merits of Jesus' sacrifice through His cross and His blood. They do not have to be baptized in water again, but they do have to acknowledge their wrong in prayer to the Creator and repent of it. The Creator has promised them that they will be released from the debt of their recent offense.

Another one of Jesus' apostles, John, as he spoke to those who had fellowship with the Creator and His Son, revealed the course of action for those who would offend in such a relationship: "If we confess our sins, He is faithful and righteous to forgive us our sins and to cleanse us from all unrighteousness" (1 John 1:9). An example of this is found in one Simon, who offended the Creator early in his new walk with Him. After Simon was converted, through belief and water baptism, he offended because he thought that the gift of the Creator's Spirit could be secured through money. As a result of this offense, Simon came under a strong rebuke through the apostle Peter:

> You have no part or portion in this matter, for your heart is not right before God. Therefore, repent of this wickedness of yours, and pray the Lord that, if possible, the intention of your heart may be forgiven you (Acts 8:21-22).

Simon, as a constituent of the people of the Creator, did not have to be baptized in water again, but he had to repent and pray in order to be released from the debt of his current offense.

The Creator's Glorious Release

We have seen the conditional release of debt by the Creator for those who are in the world and for His people who offend. But there are other dimensions of the Creator's act of extending forgiveness that can help us in our process of extending forgiveness to our debtors. A story recorded in Luke 15 helps us to appreciate the heart and disposition of the Creator regarding releasing offenders from their debts.

The story is about a father who had two sons. The younger asked his father for his share of the inheritance that had been apportioned to him. The father obliged the younger son who collected his inheritance and went to a distant country. There he squandered his inheritance by his loose living. When his money ran out, he began to be in need. So, he eventually gained employment – he fed swine. In his impoverished state, he would have gladly eaten what the swine were eating.

But being jolted to his senses, he reasoned that there was no need for him to be hungry when his father's servants had more than enough bread. He determined to return home and admit his offenses before heaven and his father and appeal to him to make him one of his hired servants. As he approached home, with his verbal script ready to present to his father, what ensued was not what he had expected.

His father saw him approaching from a distance. Feeling compassion for his son, the father ran out to meet him, and then embraced him and kissed him. The son acknowledged his wrong and spoke of his unworthiness to be called a son. The father did not comply with the son's line of reasoning but ordered that the best robe be put on him and he gave him a ring and sandals for his feet. Moreover, a fattened calf was killed, and the return of the son was celebrated. The reasoning of the father was that the son was dead but began to live again, and was lost, but he had been found.

It is the heart and actions of the father in our story that helps us to understand the heart and disposition of the Creator, as it relates to His forgiving or releasing His offenders from their debt. The first thing that can be noticed about the father, on his son's return, was that he saw the son's condition. What did he see? Perhaps, he saw the impoverished state of his son. Maybe, the father saw his son as living beneath his privileges, or he believed that the son had made a mistake with the fortune he had inherited.

Just as this father saw his son in an impoverished state, so too the Creator sees the state of want and need of those who have offended Him. He sees us in our offense, probably just as confused as the inhabitants of the city of Nineveh, who escaped His punishment because they repented of their grave offenses.

As the Creator worked with the heart of a prophet called Jonah, who had been given the assignment to preach to the people of Nineveh, He revealed His view of the offenders. He said to Jonah,

> …You had compassion on the plant for which you did not work and which you did not cause to grow, which came up overnight and perished overnight. Should I not have compassion on Nineveh, the great city in which there are more than 120,000 persons who do not know the difference between their right and left hand, as well as many animals (Jonah 4:10-11)?

Wow! In the Creator's eyes, the offenders in Nineveh were confused, as they did not know the difference between their right and left hand. Do we see our debtors in their impoverished state? Their poverty does not have to be material in nature. They may lack moral wealth or wisdom that may have resulted in them making decisions that offended others. Do we see them as confused, in the maze of life, not having a clue as to how they can extricate themselves from the quagmire of their situation? What do you see, or observe in your offender?

The father, in our story, was able to identify with the struggle of his son and felt compassion towards him. Likewise, the Creator is able to forgive His debtors because He has compassion towards them. He can identify with their struggles! As we look beyond the offense, there is usually some struggle going on in the lives of offenders. Beyond the offense, there are also the offenders' questions. This is evident in one of the encounters of Jesus during His earthly ministry. He met a Samaritan woman, and after revealing to her that the man she currently had was not her husband, she perceived that Jesus was a prophet, and subsequently uttered a spiritually-insightful statement: "Our fathers worshipped in this mountain, and you people [*the Jews*] say that in Jerusalem is the place where men ought to worship" (John 4:20).

In response, Jesus went on to reveal to her the kind of worshippers His Father seeks – those who would worship Him in spirit and in truth. This encounter helps us to understand that lurking in the background of the offense are inner conflicts and questions that occupy the cognitive spaces of the Creator's offenders. Can we appreciate the inner struggles of those who offend us?

The father running towards his returning son implies his readiness to help his son. He was ready to release his son from the offenses perpetrated against him. The Creator is also ready to release His offenders from their debt: "For You, Lord, are good, and ready to forgive, and abundant in lovingkindness to all who call upon You" (Psalm 86:5). Of course, in calling upon Him, the debtors must obey His terms or instructions, and when they do, they encounter a Creator who is already poised and willing to release them from their debts.

Restoration is what we also see as the father released his son from his debt. The best robe, ring, and sandals being placed on the feet of the son, all point to a restored relationship with the father. It also implies that his son was reinstated to his "sonship"; the father referred to the offending son, after his conversion, as his son, underscoring the reinstatement of "sonship." Mere servitude for the son was not a part of the relational equation, as far as the father was concerned.

Similarly, when the Creator forgives His debtors, they are restored to a wholesome relationship with Him. Additionally, they are reinstated as His children, His sons and daughters, as they become members of His spiritual family on earth, with all the privileges that accompany such status.

As indicated earlier, when the Creator releases the debtor from a debt, they become reconciled to Him; the hostility in the relationship, caused by the debt that accompanied the offense, is removed. Therefore, when the Creator extends forgiveness, debtors, in addition to being restored and reinstated, are also reconciled.

Here, we can see another distinction in the process of extending forgiveness for human beings and the Creator – for us, reconciliation and restoration, or reinstatement, are not always possible or advisable when we extend forgiveness. However, reconciliation and restoration, or reinstatement, are attached to the Creator's forgiveness. This is not to say that, for us, these are out of our reach. On the contrary! Reconciliation, restoration, and reinstatement, when considered from a holistic perspective, remain viable options for us when we extend forgiveness to those who have offended us.

The father celebrated the prodigal son's return home. There was joy over his renewed state; his conversion, restoration, reinstatement, and reconciliation were cause for jubilation. The celebration was spawned out of a change in the son's moral condition. The release of his debt seemed to have been triggered by the son (if we would find a context for him, he would belong to biblical national Israel or the Jews, God's people under the Old Covenant) coming to his senses and having a change of mind as he acknowledged his wrong, which was a significant turning point in his relationship with, first, heaven (the Creator) and then his father.

Today, when the Creator's debtors come to their senses, realize their offense(s) and what it is doing to their relationship with their Maker, and then become obedient to His will through repentance, this places them on a path to being released from their debts. It is the repentant spirit or individual with a heart that is willing to turn from the offensive behavior that attracts the attention of the Creator, who graciously offers release of debt:

> Thus says the Lord, 'Heaven is My throne and the earth is My footstool. Where then is a house you could build for Me? And where is a place that I may rest? For My hand made all these things, thus all these things came into being,' declares the Lord. 'But to this one I will look, to him who is humble and contrite [*repentant*] of spirit, and who trembles at My word' (Isaiah 66:1-2).

Consequently, as debtors turn to their Creator and conform to His will, He rejoices over them. Jesus reveals that, "...there is joy in the presence of the angels of God over one sinner [*offender*] who repents" (Luke 15:10).

As human beings, we can be inspired to forgive because of the change in the moral condition of our offenders, like the father in our story. Although we know that forgiving our debtors is not absolutely hinged on their moral improvement, such improvement can aid in the release of their debt, particularly as we consider the progress of some offenders who engage in wholesome interpersonal exchanges. Such moral improvements belong to what I have referred to as the fertile ground for extending forgiveness. This will be developed later in our time together.

In leaving our story of the father and the son, we move now to identify other traits of the Creator as He extends forgiveness to His offenders. One of the things we can notice in the Creator is His thoroughness when it comes to releasing His debtors from their debt that accompanied offense. As I speak to the Creator's thoroughness, pertaining to offenses, I am referring to His comprehensive release of debts regardless of their nature. Whatever debt is incurred, through a breach of the Creator's code for our lives on earth, the procured ransom payment, that is, Jesus' death on the cross, is enough for the Creator to release us from that debt.

We do not have the situation where the merit of the cross is only able to cover certain debts and not others. Rather, the merits and sufficiency of the cross is able to run the entire gamut of offenses and deal effectively with all of them. Once again, the apostle Paul, in referring to the Creator's people and His work in their lives, explains, "…He made you alive together with Him [*Jesus, the Creator's Son*], having forgiven us all our transgressions" (Colossians 2:13). The word "all" implies thoroughness or completeness about the release that debtors receive. Now, that is Good News! For us, there is great value in this particular quality in the Creator; that is, His thoroughness works effectively with all debt!

As human beings, we offend each other in various ways and at different times. Today, I may offend you with a careless, scurrilous word, and still tomorrow, I may be in debt to you because I acted out of character and cut into the parking space available to you at work, while fully cognizant that you were waiting for it first.

If you are to be inspired by the Creator's thoroughness in releasing His offenders from their debts, then it follows that, in your disposition to forgive, you will release me from the debt of that scurrilous word, as well as the parking offense. Failure to release me from one offense would place you in a position that is not congruent with the Creator's release of debts. Remember He forgives "all!" It is not easy at times, but the attainable standard of "all" is before us.

Akin to His thoroughness, with regard to releasing His debtors from their offenses, the Creator is faithful, as evidenced in His forgiving actions. Both groups of offenders can find, in the Creator, a reliable friend who, contingent upon their compliance to His terms, will release them from their debts. The Creator's people were given an assurance of this by the apostle John. If sin is present in their lives, John assures them of His forgiveness, "If we confess our sins, He [*the Creator*] is faithful and righteous to forgive us our sins and to cleanse us from all unrighteousness" (1 John 1:9). Please, do not take this, His faithfulness, as His permission to offend, but see it as the Creator's willingness to fight for, through the extension of Himself, a wholesome relationship with us human beings, the apex of His creation on earth.

How does the Creator's faithfulness, in extending forgiveness, impact our experience with extending forgiveness? What is seen in the Creator's faithfulness, in releasing debtors, is our tendency, as human beings, to incur debt, thus, failing Him. The Creator's faithfulness to forgive interacts with our propensity to own reoccurring debt (**see figure 10**).

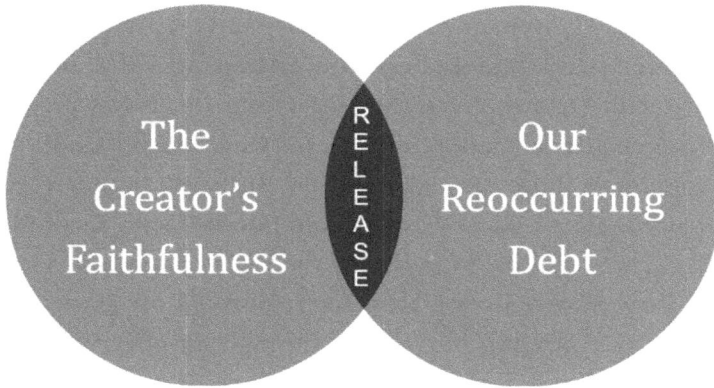

Figure 10 – *Interaction Between Faithfulness and Debt*

It can be said that in the background of the faithful disposition of the Creator is His understanding of our propensity to incur debt, through violation of His code for our behavior. This understanding is underscored in His providing for the release of the debts in both groups of offenders. Once again, this is no excuse to commit offenses or even take the license to offend, but we can gain a perspective on how things actually are: Reoccurring human debt that accompany offenses requires a Creator who is faithful and willing to pardon us.

And so, the contingent faithfulness of the Creator, in releasing debtors from their debts, can work to shape our faithfulness in releasing our debtors. It does this by helping us to understand that offenses from and towards our fellow human beings do reoccur because we all have the tendency to fail one another. Therefore, when offenses reoccur, a faithful release of debt is necessary to maintain our valuable relational connections. In faithful release we are fighting to retain our wholesome relationships!

There is one more attribute of the Creator I want to mention, as it relates to this issue of extending forgiveness. It is the fact that He is not mindful of the released debt of His debtors. To have a greater appreciation of this, one may want to understand how things were under a covenant the Creator had with the nation of Israel or the Jews. It is referred to as the First or Old Covenant. Under it, because of its ceremonial limitations, sins (offenses) were remembered year in, and year out.

Also, the Old Covenant was preliminary and preparatory in nature. In being preliminary, it preceded a new arrangement that the Creator established with His people, in the New Covenant. It was preparatory because it prepared the nation of Israel for what He did for all people, at His appointed time, through His Son. In being both preliminary and preparatory, the Old Covenant could not deal with sins (offenses) effectively. Through His Son's death, the Creator brought into existence the New Covenant, which made it possible for all people, not just the Jews, to become His people through an effective means of forgiveness of debts.

With special consideration to offenses, under the New Covenant, the debts of the Creator's people are remembered no more. This is unlike the situation of His people under the Old Covenant, where debts were remembered. In this difference, where debts are no longer remembered, one can begin to understand why the New Covenant is better than the Old.

So, for those (His people) in a covenant relationship with the Creator under the New Covenant, there is no remembering of their debts: "For I will be merciful to their iniquities and I will remember their sins no more" (Hebrews 8:12). "I will remember their sins no more," what does this mean? Primarily, this statement points to the difference between the Old and New Covenants. There was remembrance of sins (the debts) under the Old, but this is not how things are under the New. Again, the Old Covenant's ceremonial requirements could not effectively remove debts that occurred through offenses, so they were constantly before the Creator.

However, under the New Covenant, because of the effectiveness of Jesus' sacrifice and blood, debts can effectively be released; consequently, the debts through offenses are no longer before the Creator with regard to those who would embrace His will for their release.

Still, this business of the Creator not remembering His people's sins, under the splendor of the New Covenant, also reflects His cognitive treatment of their sins (debts). In this regard, the Creator does not think of, is not mindful of, has a fixture on, bring to the remembrance of, or bear in mind, the debt forgiven. He does not allow His thought processes to dwell on the debts (offenses) of His people. Surely, for those who are not His people today, their debts through offenses are cognitively ever before Him because they have not experienced the merits of the cross of Jesus; but this is not the case with His people.

This ability of the Creator to not be mindful of the debts of His people is before us as an example of how we can cognitively treat those we seek to release from their debts or offenses. It is within our capacity to not be "mindful" of an offense perpetrated against us.

The ability to "sift through" and "pick out" what we allow to occupy our thought processes is seen in Paul's letter to the Philippians, where he admonished the Creator's people with these words:

Finally, brethren, whatever is true, whatever is honorable, whatever is right, whatever is pure, whatever is lovely, whatever is of good repute, if there is any excellence and if anything worthy of praise, dwell on these things (Philippians 4:8).

The Creator then becomes a model for us! He reflects our competency in not being "mindful" of the debts of our debtors. We can choose not to dwell on them.

As we look at the Creator's attributes regarding debt release for His debtors, I have provided an illustration to help us further understand His disposition or character as He moves to release His offenders from the debts of their offenses (*see figure 11*).

In this chapter, we have taken time to identify the qualities of the Creator that are at work when He applies the merits of His Son's sacrificial death to our lives and as He releases us from the debts in our offenses. In doing so, we called attention to the conditional nature of His act of forgiveness towards His offenders. It was noted too, that this is connected to His unique functions as Lawgiver and Judge of all humankind.

Yet, as the Creator participates in releasing His debtors from their debts, we find utility in His process and in our quest and need to release our debtors from their debts. We now turn our attention further to the business of empathy. I hope that you are still buckled up!

Release of Debt

Figure 11 – *The Creator's Release Funnel*

For further deliberation…

1. The receipt of the Creator's forgiveness is conditional. For human beings, extending forgiveness is an imperative. How do we reconcile this?

2. There are two groups of the Creator's offenders and two different paths to forgiveness. Do you agree? Why or why not?

3. The offender is in an impoverished state. How might this be true?

4.   Is it all right to assume that there may be unsettled issues and unanswered questions in the lives of those who offend us? How so?

5.   As the offended considers their wellbeing, why would releasing offenders from all of their debts be an important undertaking?

6.   What is at stake in our valuable relationships if our release of debts does not keep pace with the offenses?

I Forgive

Chapter Six

The Role of Empathy in Forgiving

"In seeing him locked up, I felt so sorry for him." - **Karen Woodside**

I invite you to go with me on another excursion. This time we are going to visit a kindergarten setting. Have you ever visited such a setting? Perhaps, it was a classroom setting or just a room, filled with the tender ones running to and fro, busily engaged, with toys scattered over the floor. As we visit our classroom setting, you may see an old cast iron bathtub, set aside for the kids to sit in, as a treat, during reading time. You may also see the stains of food matter and spilled juice marring the conspicuous multicolored uniforms the tender ones are wearing.

As we observe their high energy and curious nature, the teacher summons their attention and marshals it towards us, guests for the occasion. As the tender ones give us their undivided attention, and as their gaze is fixed on us, waiting in anticipation, what do you see? I believe you may want to say something like "Hi," or "Hello everyone," but what do you see? Do you see their bright eyes, beautiful smiles, smooth skin, multi-textured hair, and the varicolored complexion of their faces? Do you see their pristine state, unspoiled by the vicissitudes of life?

What about their eagerness to hear what you and I have to say to them? Their eagerness points to their highly impressionable minds. Their brains are still developing and creating the neurological framework that would act as a kind of critical "blueprint" to help with behavioral referencing and the formulation of their worldviews. The prefrontal cortex, which is the section of our brains that helps in the decision-making process, does not fully develop until the late teenage years. So, like sponges, the brains of our tender ones are actively soaking up information that will help build their character so that they can function intellectually and socially.

As we return their gaze, we find ourselves looking into innocent faces, that is, those whose conscientiousness with regard to offenses has not yet been fully developed. They do not have a good appreciation of our mutual moral "oughtness," yet. This is not to say that they cannot offend others, and we know that they can be offended, but their view of our (the conscientious ones) world of offense is not sharp enough to keenly delineate between being offended and offending.

It is through their developmental environment, and the disciplinary guidance of responsible caregivers found in it, that our tender ones are helped in being able to perceive, with greater definition, the contours of offense, both perpetrated and received.

Regarding offenses perpetrated, prior to their consciousness, Scripture implies that the Creator has a special arrangement with our tender ones, where offenses that enter the category of sin are not imputed before Him. In a text where Jesus models the virtues of children, He admonished His auditors "…not to despise one of these little ones, for I say to you that their angels in heaven continually see the face of My Father who is in heaven" (Matthew 18:10). Also, during the earthly ministry of Jesus, children (our tender ones) were welcome by Him, and He laid His hands on them, which was a sign of His blessing upon them:

> Then some children were brought to Him so that He might lay His hands on them and pray, and the disciples rebuked them. But Jesus said, 'Let the children alone, and do not hinder them from coming to Me; for the kingdom of heaven belongs to such as these.' After laying His hands on them, He departed from there (Matthew 19:13-15).

The humble, teachable, and amenable disposition of children is elevated as a mark of those who would experience the kingdom of Jesus.

Again, it is apparent from Scripture that our tender ones are moving towards a state of consciousness and imputation or culpability for their offenses before the Creator. They transition to this state. "Exactly when?" someone may ask. It is a transition that is not the same for every tender one; you must know of the precocious ones, who seem to exhibit mature traits before their peers. Nevertheless, the transition to culpability occurs.

The apostle Paul helps us out here, as he speaks about dying at the arrival of the Creator's Law, which revealed his offense:

> I once was alive apart from the Law; but when the commandment came, sin [*offense*] became alive and I died; and this commandment, which was to result in life, proved to result in death for me; for sin, taking an opportunity through the commandment, deceived me and through it killed me (Romans 7:9-11).

The arrival of the Law/commandment was specific to Paul, that is, he became conscious about it and, consequently, he was made to be aware of his offense and its impact on his life. We can understand this because the Law/commandment that Paul says came and killed him was given hundreds of years before his birth and his writing to the Christians in Rome.

Now, let us bring focus to our gaze and look at each one of the tender ones before us. Individual in nature, with incalculable value, it is impossible for us to tell or grasp the full potential that reside within each of them. But we know that each one of them has the potential to impact our world in ways so profound that when they finish their course in life, they are missed, along with the contributions they have made. Of course, these profound ways are not limited to the revolutionary contributions of, say, a Bill Gates or Steve Jobs. They also include the contributions of a janitor or a pedestrian crossing worker.

For now, we see the tender ones in the kindergarten setting, and as we look into their faces, we see the innocent, immature, and ignorant with regard to offenses. By the way, our visit was to help inform their consciousness about the different types of flowers, from the live specimens that we brought along with us.

As our visit ends, and we leave the setting, we are overwhelmed with a sense of value and worth seen in each of the tender ones. We consider, because of such value, it is no wonder the Creator is relentless in His desire to build on His intimacy with us as human beings.

The Pristine Perspective

This pristine perspective of the tender ones (seen in their innocence, impunity, immaturity, naivety, and high value) can help the offended acquire empathy to the point where they could extend forgiveness to those who have offended them. The pristine perspective provides the offended with a picture of the offender before the offense occurs. We were all in this pristine state before our environment, with its negative elements that promote the tendency to offend, had its impact on us. It can be said that the offender was in a pristine state before the offending traits developed!

Because of the negative components in the developmental environment, offending behaviors find their gestation period within the pristine ones who then become offenders. This is easily seen in the case of some bullies and their bullying, a phenomenon that has recently been given particular focus, especially within public schools. And so, we have a big bully at school that beats up and taunts fellow students.

However, our pristine perspective says that the big bully was not always like that. He was innocent and highly impressionable before his offending traits developed. But in his environment, something was either missing, like proper discipline with its instructive elements attached to it, or added, like an offending abusive act perpetrated against him, which contributed to his anger and tendency to act out. The negative thing, missing or added, in our tender state, contributes to our offensive behaviors in our interpersonal relationships, as conscious culpable adults.

Something missing in our developmental and even adult years also leaves us in a state of ignorance. This can be very costly or have a negative impact on our lives, regarding our relationship with both the Creator and our fellow human beings. Yet, ignorance is not an excuse to commit a culpable offensive act.

Because sometimes we do not know: 1) the better option; 2) all of the details of the situation; 3) that we are acting offensively; 4) the feelings or perspectives of others; and, 5) the negative ramifications attached to our behavior, there is a tendency to offend. Ignorance in the offender, therefore, should factor in significantly in the move towards empathy.

Another important consideration is the Creator's assistance to those who are ignorant but demonstrate a desire for Him and His will for their lives. He works to enlighten the ignorant: "And without faith, it is impossible to please Him, for he who comes to God must believe that He is and that He is a rewarder of those who seek Him" (Hebrews 11:6).

A Peek Down the Road

We have taken a retrospective look at the offender, through our kindergarten setting; it is fitting for us to project a bit, as we examine the offender as they travel down the road of life and through the passage of time. One thing that is constant and reliable as time passes is change. The offender is not exempted from it. So, the goal here is to try and imagine or envision how the offender will be impacted by change that is concomitant with the passing of time. Such projection can help us acquire empathy, which is so important to possess if we wish to extend forgiveness to those who offend us.

Sure, you know the offender now as cold and callous. Or you may see them as selfish and abrasive in their arrogance and disregard for the feelings and concerns of others. But why not take a few minutes and project an image of them a few years along the road of life? The image should also reflect the natural changes in the offender's body, as the aging process occurs. What do you see? Do you see the possibility of the offender finally reaching an understanding that their offensive words or behavior impeded the harmonious interpersonal relationship they might have had with you? That if they could turn back the hands of time, they would not have said or done it?

I know of a man who, because of his uncontrolled lust and proclivity, was unfaithful to his devoted wife. They had accomplished much together, inclusive of a number of business enterprises in prominent locations, several pieces of land, and a home. Finally, his wife, who had had enough, decided to divorce him. A few years "down the road of life," and looking at what he had lost because of his offending behavior, he uttered these words, "I regret what I did." By then, it was too late, in his case, for reconciliation. His ex-wife had remarried, and another man began to enjoy the fruits of their labor.

Perhaps, you may be saying at this juncture, "He deserved what he got," or "He had it coming." I know, "I get that," as one of my university professors used to say. Surely, he did not help the situation with his proclivities. Yet, the possibility of the offender coming to their senses, through regret, has some utility for us in reaching the point of empathy.

Again, "stupid forgiveness" is not being advocated here, where there is a disregard for the many parts that are connected to extending forgiveness. However, because we know that forgiving the offender is primarily for the offended, the process is a helpful one, as he or she would mull over the possibility of the offender eventually taking a new positive position or perspective on the matter.

Do you see the offenders needing others down the road, as the winds of change blow in their lives? What about when old age sets in, with its complications? How about sickness in the body cutting in and humbling the ones who are filled with arrogance, that is, the ones who believe that they do not need anyone and, without care, forge ahead with the offending action, anyway? What about when offenders come to a state of dependency on others?

We are visiting such a projection on offenders, not to respond with possible vindictiveness, but to garner a perspective of their vulnerability, finiteness, fragility, and dependability, which they may not see, perhaps, because of their selfishness or foolish pride. Again, their developmental environments have had a significant impact on the behavior of offenders. It is possible that they may have lacked something in their external environment, or something negative may have been added in their earlier years that led to such offensive acts. Whatever the case, they may eventually regret their offensive words and/or actions.

Pervasive Offense

As we understand the fallible nature of both the offender and offended this aids our empathy. An honest look at ourself will reveal that there is a certain possibility that we offended someone today or may do so down the road of life. Notwithstanding that the offense may not be in the same category of those perpetrated against us, nevertheless, we are all potential offenders. Therefore, the possibility of offending another is something that is not too far from any of us.

How does this perspective help our participatory understanding of the feelings of others, specifically, those of an offender? In acknowledging that they offended me today, but I may offend them tomorrow, the question to ask is, "How would I want to be treated, if I offend someone?" Realizing that "the table of offense" can easily turn, a similar question can also be asked, "Okay, now that I have perpetrated a grievous offense, would I want the offended to respond in kind?" The answers to these questions can be "pulled" from the future into the present as they can help shape how we respond to the offender in the here and now.

When the offended becomes the offender, possible answers to the above two questions are: "I want to be treated with respect"; "I want the offended to see that I had the best of intentions"; "He must know that I was not my usual self – I had a bad day"; "She surely must realize that that was not all there is to me"; and, "That was just my first strike, three strikes and I am out, right?"

The idea here is this: We want to transpose the same way we would want to be treated by those we offend to those who have offended us. If you are thinking about that familiar Scripture, "In everything, therefore, treat people the same way you want them to treat you, for this is the Law and the Prophets" (Matthew 7:12), then without doubt, it has relevancy.

Project Love

Being empathetic towards an offender, on the path towards extending forgiveness, necessitates that we stop to try and understand where love fits into the process. Really, the stop is indispensable! The word love has been used to describe how we feel about a lot of things, especially in the English language. Context should be considered in order to understand the significance and intent of its use. Surely, "I love ice-cream" does not carry the same significance as, "I love my car," or "I love my spouse."

Love then is an intriguing word that pulls us in, to the point that we desire to know more about it. While it is important to our matter at hand, love is applicable in every dimension of our interpersonal relations.

But before we can see how it impacts empathy towards an offender, we need to have a clearer picture of what love is. Beyond "I love ice-cream," Scripture delineates for us what love is:

> Love is patient, love is kind and is not jealous; love does not brag and is not arrogant, does not act unbecomingly; it does not seek its own, is not provoked, does not take into account a wrong suffered, does not rejoice in unrighteousness, but rejoices with the truth; bears all things, believes all things, hopes all things, endures all things (1 Corinthians 13:4-7).

We cannot deal exhaustively with such a love, as mentioned in the Scripture verses above. However, our subject matter necessitates that we take somewhat of a peek into it. It is very important to point out too that the Creator is characterized by such love; He exudes it towards people! To speak about love is to speak of the Creator. Like that compass that always points to the geographical north, so it is that when love becomes the subject of our conversation, it points to the Creator. He embodies and epitomizes love; if there is any struggle with it, we do well to move towards Him for understanding, help, clarity, and courage in manifesting it.

With specific reference to becoming more empathetic towards releasing the offender from their debt, love, revealed in patience, is indispensable! The offense occurred, but tolerance or forbearance towards the offender allows love to gain traction. To be patient, is to love! In patience, we are not condoning the offense, but we are enduring the person because we understand that there is a distinction between the offender and the offense. In such an understanding, the offense does not encapsulate the offender.

Through patience, and thus love, notwithstanding the offense, an encounter with the "last nerve" is indefinitely delayed. I do believe you are familiar with individuals who say, "She is getting on my last nerve," or "He is getting on my last nerve." Such expressions are typically precursors to "I have had enough!" of the person, which could then lead to some retaliatory eruption. Perhaps, you are more familiar with the offensive experience becoming "the straw that broke the camel's back." However, I humbly submit to you, that with patience, the last nerve and straw are hard to find.

Patience, in this enterprise of love, provides a seat along the thoroughfare of our reasoning capacity for belief and hope, to "sit" with the perspective that things could change for the better. It also provides the stretch or flexibility needed to endure character flaws, as people mature towards the ideal of harmonious interpersonal relations.

In the functionality of love, there is an enduring of the offense, not a condoning of it or an enabling of it. Through love, the pain of the hurtful offense is absorbed! Are you still buckled up? Scripture reveals that love covers a multitude of offenses. This view of love is help by the picture of a marathon runner, who suffers a shin fracture during a significant race. Yet, to experience the honor and glory attached to finishing, he runs on even though he is in agony.

Within reason, the runner realizes that his body could endure the pain of the moment for the greater glory. Similarly, enduring the pain in the hurt of an offense has an objective: to align us with the offender in seeking to understand their state with the prospect of making a positive difference in the interpersonal relationship. One can endure the pain of the offense because of love; it is a kind of investment, which can have great relational returns.

Not only does love find traction through patience or endurance, but it also finds its way through kindness, that is, that gift of mercy that we allow to be meted out from the heart towards our offenders, although they do not deserve it. From a practical perspective, it is similar to an employee making a cup of coffee for the boss who just, "chewed them out," or a father providing a place to sleep for a drug-addicted son, who earlier stole the rent money to feed his addiction. This may be difficult to accept, but when we are offended, we are still holding a "bag" of kindness: It is still in our hands in the wake of an offense! Is there any mercy left in your "bag" to give to the offender?

Now, there is one dimension of love that directly reflects the process of extending forgiveness, and that is, it keeps no record of wrong. When we do not tabulate the offenses perpetrated against us, we are functioning in love. Again, we are possibly treating those who have offended us, as though they never did; there is no holding on to the score of the offense for an opportune time to "throw" it in the offender's face. Really, the edifying character of love that builds up individuals, and not break them down, takes away the notion of keeping the score for the right time, with a view towards "getting even."

We have taken a closer look at some of the attributes of love, namely: patience, kindness, endurance, and not keeping a record of wrong! These are essential features that can help to move the offended along the process to the point of empathy and extending forgiveness. Through these noble qualities of love, the offended is wonderfully positioned to acquire an understanding of the feelings of their offender, which then makes it easier for them to release the debt.

Undiminished Value

I am amazed at the Creator's wisdom and power. Springtime is an amazing time of the year, and these attributes of His have an opportunity to shine. In springtime, the trees are budding, and the flowers are blooming. Even the grass is growing. Have you ever stopped and looked at a patch of wild grass or weeds growing in front of you? What variety is on display, from the clovers to the dandelions! It is just amazing to consider all of the different configurations needed for all plant life to survive, reproduce, sustain man and wildlife, and for each species to maintain its distinctiveness.

While plants and trees hold a certain value, we also see value in the animal kingdom. Cattle, horses, goats, sheep, deer, and even possums, all have a certain value reposed within them by the Creator. And how can I leave out dogs and cats, which sometimes seem to hold more value than human beings in the way they are treated (let the reader be aware that I am not advocating animal neglect or cruelty)?

I can recall a report regarding a wealthy woman who left a multi-million-dollar estate to a cat. We will not go further down this line of thought because I think you see that we can repose too much value on animals so much so that it can reach inappropriate proportions. This is not to take away from the significance of pets and the crucial part they play in helping, supporting, comforting, and protecting us, especially the elderly.

However, value, worth, or significance takes on a different dimension when it comes to man himself. Here, man is gender-neutral, as I am referring to both males and females. The value of man is greater than that of plants, trees, the beasts of the field, and our precious pets. Man can be described as the apex of the Creator's creation on earth. This is seen in man's mastery over his environment; sometimes, however, this extends too far, and he destroys what he has been entrusted with. Yet, dominion of his environment, inclusive of animal and plant life, demonstrates that man's value is phenomenal.

A clearer understanding of man's value is seen in the fact that, unlike other life forms on earth, man has been created in the image and likeness of his Creator:

Then God said, 'Let Us make man in Our image, according to Our likeness; and let them rule over the fish of the sea and over the birds of the sky and over the cattle and over all the earth, and over every creeping thing that creeps on the earth (Genesis 1:26).

This portion of Scripture holds man up as uniquely different in value than any other thing or creature on the earth.

Man, has been given something special by the Creator which allows him to think, decide, judge, create, consider, ponder, engage in, disengage from, build, seek, wait, watch, reflect, rule, love, hate, become tentative, polite, courteous, curious, respectful, compassionate, and empathetic. He can act sensibly and conscientiously, far above the animals. Man has been given a spirit that is made in the image of his Creator. Man's spirit is the invisible part of man that is designed to reflect the Creator and be in communion with Him. Man's spirit also helps him to govern his mutual moral "oughtness."

Indeed, man is valuable from conception to the grave. However, his value is obscured because of his offensive acts. Sometimes the offense hides the value of the offender, but their value is still in its place! I am not a sporting enthusiast at this stage in my life. However, I had the rare opportunity to watch Super Bowl 50, with some friends. The match-up was between the Denver Broncos and the Carolina Panthers. Initially, I did not have a favorite team that I wanted to win; however, I soon found myself pulling for the Panthers. I backed the wrong team! The Panthers lost the game; the defense of the Broncos was phenomenal. I did not lose any sleep over the outcome!

The Broncos' defense was phenomenal, but that was not all that caught my attention during the game. The Broncos' player, #21, Aqib Talib, also featured prominently because, early in the game, he seemed to have been, in my view, "a loose cannon" making misstep after misstep. He seemed to have been an embarrassment to the Broncos. At one point, I believe I even questioned why the head coach of the Broncos was allowing him to stay in the game. Talib was allowed to stay in the game, right up to its end.

Was the head coach on to something that escaped my attention while I watched Talib for the first time? Did he have an appreciation for something in Talib that was beyond his missteps? Was there something in Talib that was still intact that made it possible for his negative behavior to be endured but not condoned by the coach? You know the answer to these questions, don't you? Yes, there was something – it was Talib's value to the Broncos and the Super Bowl game. But beyond that, it was his value as a human being. The missteps blinded my sight to Talib's value, but not the coach's. Why did I point this out? I am hoping that my experience would help us to look beyond the missteps or offenses of others and consider the greater dimensions of offenders, which are inherently part of their value.

The depth, height, width, and length of man's dexterity and proficiency prohibit us from placing him in a "pigeon hole" regarding his value. It prohibits us from seeing our fellow human beings through some single function or experience that may be characterized by ineptitude or proficiency in the human endeavor. Really, outside behavioral experiences, offensive or otherwise, man's value is inherently intact. Before the action, his value is in its place. It is found in that which constitutes the full garment of what makes human beings who they are in terms of gender, cognitive capacity, sexuality, physical stature, emotional resources, and spiritual dimension.

Still, in the realm of sports, I can recall an athletic senior in high school. We will call him Bruce. Bruce's school was small, in terms of faculty and student population. At one time there was even talk of closing it because of its size. When it came down to playing sports, you had the same students moving from one sport to the next. Bruce and his teammates would move from playing football to basketball and then to baseball; you get the idea.

However, I noticed something about Bruce, as I trekked his performance across those sporting events. Bruce was on the "B-team" when he was playing basketball. On the "B-team" he did not see much playing time, like those on the "A-team." But when Bruce played another sport, baseball, he shined. He was on the "A-team" when it came to playing baseball. He was in the pitching lineup and, indeed, was an impressive pitcher; he played first base; and, he batted regularly. He featured prominently in baseball, but not so much in basketball.

Why did we visit Bruce's athletic experiences? To help us see that one's worth and value is too great to be defined by a single failure or series of failures or by mediocre performance in a particular endeavor. In such failings and mediocre showings, value seeks an opportunity to shine, as evident in the case of Bruce's baseball proficiency.

Turning to offenses, this view helps us to understand that the "cable" connecting value to our offenders still holds despite their offending actions. The offender's value does not diminish, notwithstanding the offense. As gold, in the heart of the earth, is marred by dirt and other impurities, so it is that the value of the offender is marred by the offense. But value is still inherently a part of the offender, just as value is attached to gold, even though encrusted by the earth in its unrefined state.

Becoming empathetic towards someone who has offended us is significantly helped when we recognize their great value that has been marred by the offense but is still pretty much a part of them. Human value, like our shadow, is difficult to deny or disregard because it is inherently attached to what constitutes who we are.

Filtering

With a deliberate move to identify positive traits in the offender, a state of empathy can be reached and be seen as a step towards releasing an offender from their debt. In a process that I refer to as filtering, the positive qualities of the offender are separated from the negative ones. If we look close enough, we can find positive qualities in others, even as we observe their negative qualities. Even Esau had some positive attributes with him, as he plotted to kill Jacob, his brother. For, he suspended his diabolical intentions out of respect for his father, Isaac.

This filtering process serves a multi-faceted purpose. In addition to helping the offended identify good qualities within the offender, which should be affirmed and fortified, the process also serves to shine a spotlight on the areas of the relationship that need intentional focus, that is, the negatives. As focus is placed on the negatives, parties in a relationship can engage each other in a meaningful way, as they attempt to work through their issues.

During the filtering process, it should not be a surprise that the offended will conclude that the offender's positive qualities outweigh their negative traits. Therefore, the conclusion can be made that all is not bad; they (the offender) need help in a few areas. This is the case because, as human beings, good and admirable qualities are typically more copious than those that are negative and crippling to interpersonal relationships.

You are probably more familiar with the exercise given to an individual, in a problematic relationship, who is asked to make two lists by writing down the positive qualities, the pros, found in the relationship, as well as the negative, the cons. They are then asked to compare the lists. A similar exercise is experienced in this filtering process. Through the filtering process, the offended takes an inventory of what they have in their relationship with the offender; an example is provided *in figure 12*. After identifying and affirming the positives in the relationship, the offended finds courage to release the offender from their debt and the desire to work further with them, through the experience of empathy. *Figure 13* gives us a visual image of the contributors to empathy mentioned above.

We have come to understand that empathy plays a very important role as the offended releases the offender from their debt. There are several factors that we have considered that will help us develop the emotion of empathy towards the offender. These factors include, love, which can be seen as an indispensable, experiential decision – love is a decision; environmental considerations, which directs us to the negative thing added or missing during our developmental years; and, the pristine condition that necessitates us envisioning the offender in their impressionable, innocent or tender state. Our time together now takes us to a place that can help us identify favorable conditions that facilitate the release of the offender's debt.

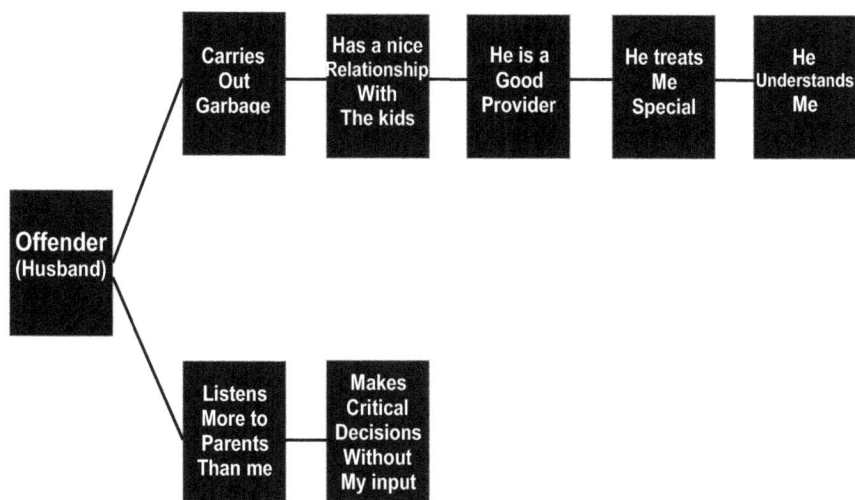

Figure 12 – *The Filtering Process*

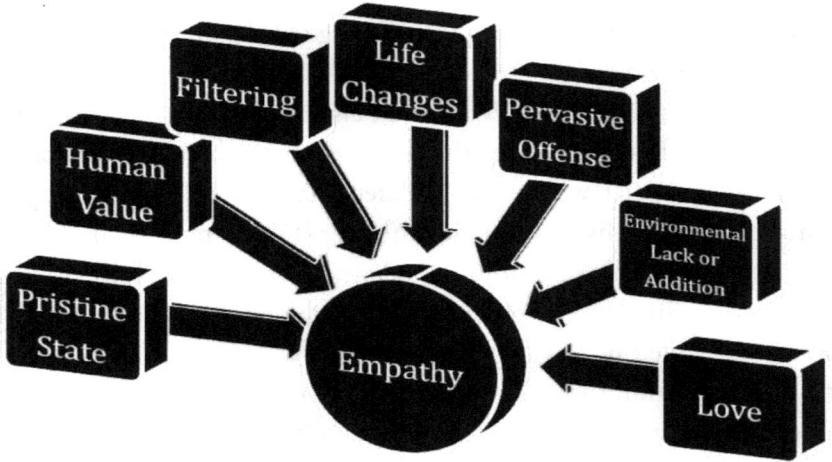

Figure 13 – *Contributors to Empathy*

For further deliberation…

1. What does the image of both the offender and the offended, in their innocent or tender state, hold for us when it comes to extending forgiveness?

2. When offended, how important is it to treat others the way you would like to be treated? Why?

3. Each one of us holds a "bag" of mercy; do you agree with this? Why or why not?

4. Why is it significant to see the offender's inherent value in the steps towards empathizing with them?

5. What is necessary to look beyond the offense and see that the offender also has positive qualities?

Chapter Seven

Fertile Ground for
Extending Forgiveness

*"I received a letter from him that spoke to the good times that we had together." - **Karen Woodside***

Extending forgiveness sometimes can be very difficult. However, the process can be significantly aided because of the encouraging disposition of offenders. Those who have an amicable spirit, which manifests behavior that augur well for mending breaches in interpersonal relationships, can help the offended in their inclination to release them from their debts. At the other end of the behavioral spectrum, the process is frustrated and made difficult for those offended when there is arrogance, lack of regard, and care or sensitivity demonstrated by offenders in their offense. While there can be behaviors perpetrated by offenders that work to perpetuate the hurt, pain, and disharmony associated with offenses, there can also be behaviors that are significant in making debt release easier.

This is the case even when we consider the acts of the Creator. There are certain qualities in those who at one time offended Him that attract Him to them, regarding the release of their debt:

'Thus says the Lord, Heaven is My throne and the earth is My footstool. Where then is a house you could build for Me? And where is a place that I may rest? For My hand made all these things. Thus, all these things come into being,' declares the Lord. 'But to this one I will look, to him who is humble and contrite of spirit, and who trembles at My word' (Isaiah 66:1-2).

Note the qualities found in the Creator's offenders that get His attention: *humility, a contrite spirit* (a repentant attitude), and *a trembling at His word* (a regard for its authority). When the Creator is attracted to us, then His blessings, including the release of our debts, are near.

We will now look at some behaviors or qualities that can assist those offended to release offenders from their debts.

Admission, the Harbinger of Accord

Acknowledgment plays a vital role in helping to move an alcoholic down the path of meaningful recovery. Admitting an offense can also improve the interpersonal relationship between the offended and the offender. Offenses occurring within a relationship suggest that something may be wrong with its dynamics or that it needs to improve or grow in a particular area. A clearer picture of the relationship is provided when the offender admits to the offended that they have committed an offense.

A false veneer of integrity that might characterize a relationship can be gotten rid of when the relational reality is defined more accurately between parties, as the offender acknowledges offense and pretense. For any relationship to flourish or move towards the ideal of harmony, regarding interpersonal exchanges, a clearer picture of its state of affairs is needed by all parties concerned; the offender's acknowledgment of an offense helps to provide such clarity. Even if the relationship with the Creator is to move forward or in the right direction, man must first admit his wrong or own up to his ill-conceived behavior(s).

So, there is something commendable when an offender acknowledges their offense to the offended. While such acknowledgment signals a certain level of maturity in the offender, it can directly impact, in a positive way, their interpersonal relationship.

Notwithstanding the offensive deed done or word spoken, the acknowledgment provides an opportunity for a pivot in the trajectory of a relationship. Because of the offender's acceptance of the offense, the ground of relational strain can be broken up so that the seeds of healing, accord, and positive differences can have an easier time to sprout and grow.

When the offended hears the offender admit, "I shouldn't have done that, I apologize," or "I was wrong in making that comment, I am sorry," "the ball is in the court" of the offended, and this has a direct bearing on their volition. Consequently, the offended may ask the question, "What am I going to do with John's acknowledgment of his offense?" This would not be inconsistent with those offended capacity to exercise their freewill. When the ball is in their court, they can help redirect the relationship so that it could become a harmonious one. Such redirecting can occur because the offended decides to release the offender, who acknowledges offense(s), from their debt.

Verbal Request

Our friends, the Nigerians, often ask, "Please, can you find room in your heart to forgive me?" This helps to reveal to the offended that the offender can have a heart that not only implies the admission of wrong, but also one that may value and desire the relationship they had prior to the offense. The appeal also suggests that room or space can exist in the heart of the offended, which could be cordoned off, especially for the release of the offender from their debt.

The verbal appeal showcased above indicates another characteristic of our ground that is conducive for releasing offenders from their debts. It can be heard in several arrangements such as:

> Forgive me, please? I just want you to know that I would greatly appreciate it if you could overlook my actions last night? Please pardon my rudeness; give me another chance? Is it possible for us to move beyond what happened the other day? I did not mean what I said; can we start over? This is difficult for me, but I promise you that it will not happen again if you would only look beyond my mistake?

Such verbal appeals directly provide the offended with a viable option, notwithstanding the context of the offense, in releasing an offender from their debt(s). This viability is primarily grounded in an offender's heart that is usually genuine and means what is verbally uttered from it. I know that sometimes it is difficult to tell the difference between a genuine or authentic heart and one that is fraudulent, even though one hears similar verbal utterances from both hearts. However, it is sometimes easy to do. This becomes obvious, when the offended has had a history with the offender, and knows their character, habits, and tendencies.

The Non-verbal Request

The verbal appeal of the offender, who asks the offended to release them from their debt, will move the process of extending forgiveness along. But we must not forget that such a request can also manifest itself in non-verbal behaviors. In a real sense, the offender's actions can "speak" louder than their words. Indeed, for the offended to embrace an appeal for release, whether verbal or non-verbal, it is essential that they own an attitude that is non-rigid, flexible, and open to the appeal, regardless of how it manifests itself.

Again, I bring to our attention the biblical character Jacob. We know about his offensive treachery when he stole Esau's blessing. Many years had gone by since they had last seen each other, and here we join them, as they are about to reunite. Jacob fears the meeting because he learns that Esau is coming to meet him with four hundred men. However, his fear did not immobilize him from acting in a manner that fostered healing in the brothers' broken interpersonal relationship.

Apparently, Jacob was genuinely sorry for what he had done to Esau. This is implied by the many animals (as gifts), which were quite valuable, that he had sent to Esau, ahead of their meeting. Additionally, when the brothers had each other in sight, and as they moved towards one another, Jacob bowed himself repeatedly before Esau. They embraced for a long time before verbal conversation ensued.

What was conspicuously absent in the conversation was a verbal appeal from Jacob. He did not ask Esau to forgive him or release him from the debt that came through the offense. However, the appeal was there in Jacob's non-verbal actions. It was "heard" in the giving of animals, the bowing down, and the protracted emotional embrace. All of these implied that Jacob was appealing to Esau, requesting his forgiveness.

The non-verbal actions of Jacob also reveal that he carried the burden of his and Esau's broken relationship. He owned up to the part he played that led to their fractured familial ties. Also, he wanted their relationship to be healed.

I am not suggesting that an offender's verbal appeal for forgiveness does not have merit. On the contrary, to hear the offender's heart in a verbal appeal for forgiveness is very important. I am simply pointing out that the appeal can manifest itself in the positive non-verbal behavior(s) of the offender, and this, too, is significant.

Its importance is not only seen in the efforts of the offender as they attempt to heal the breach in their interpersonal relationship, but it is also crucial in post-relational healing and forgiveness. Positive non-verbal behavior, seen in offenders, which requests and promotes forgiveness, should be seen in them after forgiveness. In this view, the non-verbal appeal takes on a transcending quality that works to maintain the relational gains.

To put it succinctly: The non-verbal request for forgiveness should not be discounted or scorned by the offended who, through it and their volition, can decide to release the offender from their debt(s).

In recognizing the offender's non-verbal appeal for release of their debt(s), the offended can help the offender in the process of seeking forgiveness. This is especially the case with offenders who are not used to or comfortable with the whole idea of seeking forgiveness verbally.

In one sense, although the offended may not have the verbal appeal for the release of the debt from the offender, yet the non-verbal appeal from them reveals that all is not lost when it comes to relational healing. The appeal can suggest to the offended that something occurred, notwithstanding the offense, which points to the fact that the relationship is of significance to the offender.

 Moreover, the offender's non-verbal appeal can be viewed as a positive start that can eventually morph into a more complete verbal appeal for forgiveness.

Today, far removed from the historical account of Esau and Jacob, how may such non-verbal appeals, from offenders, manifest themselves? Just as there are many relational dynamics, so too, there are many non-verbal ways offenders can appeal for forgiveness.

In a relationship between a husband and wife, the offender may be seen getting up early in the morning with a specific objective to prepare breakfast for the offended. In the relationship between a parent and a child, where the latter is the offender, he or she may complete household tasks for a week without being asked to do so. In the case of the former, when the parent is the offender, he or she may seek forgiveness by hugging the child or treating them to their favorite home-cooked meal.

By identifying the positive behavior of offenders in the above relational dynamics and similar scenarios, it is hoped that the offended can be encouraged to develop a sensitivity to the non-verbal appeals and, subsequently, find it easier to release the offender from their debt(s).

The Import of Commitment

Human beings tend to fight for what they hold as dear and valuable to them. Show me a husband who is doing all that he can to help his wife fight pancreatic cancer, aiding her with dietary changes, or the acquisition of medicinal oils, and I will show you a man that treasures his relationship with a woman who has given birth to his children, and has been his business companion and helper through the years.

Show me a student who juggles a demanding set of university courses while working arduously at a part-time job to pay for her educational expenses, all the while getting by on an average of three hours sleep per night, and I will show you an individual who is fighting to secure a foundation for a valuable career.

At the backdrop of the challenging situations mentioned above is commitment! The husband is committed to his wife; therefore, he fights for her health and wellbeing. The student is committed to self-improvement; consequently, she fights to acquire the bestowals of academia. There is something virtuous about commitment; it sustains a good fight, pursuit, and/or a relationship that functions in the ideal.

Additionally, good relationships are comprised of individuals who are loyal to their relational ties. Such loyalty manifests itself during good and bad times, in the expected and unexpected, through a rebuke and a compliment, and through the natural physiological changes imposed on us by the effects of time. A good relationship also supports and encourages while providing a platform for deepening meaningful intimacy.

Commitment can also be beneficial in that it can help the offended to release the offender from a debt that came along with an offense. As the offended observes the offender's dedication to and resilience towards the relationship, before, through, and beyond the offense, the perception of a disposition that encourages the release of the debt can develop. Implicitly, the offender, in relational commitment, states to the offended that, "Although I have messed up, by behaving in such a way, the value of our relationship transcends my unwise behavior, so I am not willing to relinquish what we have."

With such commitment, the offended is given a measure of assurance that the offender might be ready and willing to do what is necessary to put the relationship back on sound footing, even if the process may encounter a few setbacks. We know that while moving towards a goal (in this regard, that of relational healing), in many of our human endeavors, frustration and setbacks can cross our path; however, because of our commitment and perseverance, the goal can eventually be reached.

The offender's commitment to the relationship is one clear sign that they may be ready to adjust for the good of the relationship. This relational commitment then becomes a message to the offended that the relationship, although impacted by an offense, can move in a positive direction. Therefore, it is a message that can promote the release of the debt.

Maturing Growth

Still, in looking beyond the offense, the offender's maturity can also help them secure the release of their debt(s). To offend is one thing, but to develop character from such an offense is another. As the offender learns from the missteps in the relationship and adjusts their behavior, the offended is provided with the impetus to help move them beyond the pain of the offense.

In such adjustments, there is the offender's reasonableness and acceptance when the offense is presented and brought into focus. Also, there is a willingness on behalf of the offender to effect a positive change in their behavior. The offender has regard for what matters in the relationship and to the offended. There are intentional strides made to not offend again in the word or behavior that caused the relationship to be troubled in the first place. Consequently, likely, the offender will not be complacent, indifferent, or apathetic about the offensive act. There is no resignation in, "This is who I am, and if you don't like it, you can do the next best thing." Instead, the offender moves to remove the "cancer in the relationship through an introspective look at themselves. Then, there is a resolve to make a positive change.

These are parts of the maturation process, which indicates to the offended that the relationship can change for the better, despite the offender's grievous offense. The perception and reality of the offender's growth, inclusive of moral considerations, can act to move the offended along the process of releasing their debt(s).

The Jewel of Consistency

There is an expression that I "picked up" during my formative years, precisely from where I cannot recall. It goes like this, "O consistency, thou art a jewel!" The expression conveys the idea that there is value attached to the continuity of specific thoughts, teachings, and, more specifically, to our current cause, behaviors. Given the offender's consistent behavioral change, in keeping with their resolve to alter the offensive behavior perpetrated in the relationship, the offended can become more willing to extend forgiveness and release the offender from their debt(s).

This continuity in the offender's positive resolve and behavior can move the relationship along the path of healing and renewal. Consider, "Can you please forgive me, I won't do it again?" followed up with action that builds the relationship, instead of tearing it down. And consider pleasant words that foster peace, instead of those that are putrid and nasty. This indicates that change is consistent and that the relationship is moving in a positive direction.

Such continuity also works to restore the trust level that might have sustained great damage over the troubling offensive period. Relational security, marked by the parties in the relationship looking after the interests of each other, is one of the features of a healthy, stable relationship.

This security is partly based on trust. However, when it is injured, a relationship will not function optimally. The good news is that, even though wounded, confidence or trust can be restored.

When the offended observes congruency between the offender's committed determination and change in their behavior, trust has an opportunity to be restored and developed, which can then bring their relationship to the point of renewal. The possibility of the restoration of trust can also encourage the offended to release the offender from their debt(s).

Justice and Lessons

The role of justice also features prominently, as we consider the fertile ground that is useful for extending forgiveness. With certain offenses, such as those that involve a breach in societal laws, there are resulting "restitutional" consequences that require the payment of fines, community service, and/or even spending time in prison. After paying, serving or experiencing jail or prison time, the offender may feel a sense of relief given that they understand that their debt has been paid to society. Not only this, in some cases, there might be engendered in offenders a feeling that the lesson has been learned. For some, there is a resolve not to commit the grievous act again.

Additionally, other offenses may not rise to the level that requires society to exact justice. However, they still result in offenders having to "pay" in some way, for the wrong they have done, particularly with regard to their interpersonal relationships. Such offenders may also learn from the consequences of their actions. For instance, lessons can be learned through the loss of a job that may result in difficulties for the family because the offender blurted out some ill-advised words or acted improperly while at work.

Similarly, through the lack of proper prioritization of precious resources, the offensive behavior may result in difficulties for all concerned. We see this in the situation where a father spends all of his paycheck on a lotto game, even though he knew that the house mortgage was due and foreclosure was imminent, only to be disappointed when he finds out that he did not "win the lottery."

However, the "payments" exacted through the job and house losses, in the above circumstances, still brought with them their instructive components, and the offenders can still learn their lessons, even though it may be a bit too late for situational change. Whether an offender's offense rises to the level of societal restitution or some other level, because of the nature of an offense, notwithstanding "repayment," sometimes it is difficult to release them from the debt.

The offended can recognize, particularly in the case of an offender who has adapted positively through their offense, that repayment or justice has already been meted out to them. And, by demonstrating a real sense of empathy, it can be asked, "Haven't they suffered enough for their folly?" Hopefully, you are able to answer "Yes" instead of "No," as you consider your offender's "payments," and as you move towards releasing them from the debt(s).

It must be underscored that the offended needs to be very perceptive to apprehend the above behaviors or qualities found within the offender and in the fertile ground that will help them release the offender from their debt(s). Therefore, focus on, and a study of behaviors and words emanating from the offender is critical. It must also be underscored that extending forgiveness, because of an offense experienced, is not absolutely hinged to our fertile ground. Remember, forgiveness can be extended outside the actions or lack thereof, of the offender.

For further deliberation...

1. Is an admission of wrong in a relationship liberating?

2. The offended needs flexibility to be sensitive to both verbal and non-verbal requests for forgiveness from the offender. How does this quality relate to a willingness to forgive?

3. Parties who are committed to a relationship reveal the value of it! Do you agree? Why or why not?

4. If the offender is aggressively dealing with their offensive behavior so that it would not negatively impact the relationship any further, what does this tell you about their views of the relationship?

5. A verbal "Please forgive me"? and behavioral change are critical considerations when an offense occurs in a relationship! For relational harmony though, is it both/and or either/or?

Chapter Eight

Forgiving Self

"He was abusing my daughter right under my nose, and I was not aware of it!" - **Karen Woodside**

Earlier, we revealed that not only could the offended be encaged by the disposition and emotion of unforgiveness, but so can the offender. As the weight of their betrayal or offensive behavior bears down upon them, psychologically, offenders can become mentally and emotionally unsettled.

Do you remember Jacob, who feared the reunion with his brother, Esau? He felt uneasy because he knew he had offended him. However, it is implied that he experienced mental calm when he understood Esau released him from his debt. Their cooperation and cordial relationship, post the offense and reunion, point to an easing of Jacob's fear of his brother and the psychological burden he carried for so many years.

Jacob accepted the release of his debt, and he and his brother, Esau, moved on with their lives.

Some offenders, however, continue to experience psychological encaging or burden, even post-release of their debts by those they have offended. The guilt of the offense lingers longer than it is supposed to, resulting in several impairments for such individuals.

For them, there is impaired functionality, and there can exist a continuous or intermittent self-punishment because of their failure to forgive themselves. This could also lead to impeding depression, confusion concerning relationships, and shifting interests, where the things once regarded as noble and beneficial are no longer pursued.

In some cases, with the offended, there is a tendency to blame themselves for what was done to them. This is inappropriate and can lead to a struggle to forgive self for the misappropriated wrongdoing.

This is implied in Karen Woodside's lament of what took place "...
right under my nose...." In others, this inappropriate struggle to forgive self may be intimated in the questions, "How could I have been
so stupid?" and "What have I done wrong?" Or the expression, "I was
taken for a ride!" And, even as the self-blame is inappropriate in such
cases, failure to forgive self can also impair functionality and result in
the punishment of *the self.*

In the process of forgiveness, healing for both the offended and offender is of great importance, and where it is incomplete, functionality
can be hindered. In the case of offenders, healing can be incomplete or
impeded because they have not released themselves from their debts,
even though those offended might have released them and moved on
in life. Also, when there is nothing else that can be done to influence a fractured relationship, healing can be incomplete for offenders,
particularly, as they become too critical of themselves in view of their
ill-conceived behavior. Such criticism can prevent them from functioning authentically from *the self* that is or can be.

In a real sense, failure to forgive themselves and all that accompanies it becomes for some offenders a kind of "self-sanctioned" punishment for the offenses perpetrated. They make such comments as, "I
deserve it!" So, they continue to hold themselves responsible for their
offensive behaviors. Some acknowledge that they find it difficult to
forgive themselves: "I can't forgive myself!" There is a definite struggle
between the process of healing and the enduring self-punishment in
failing to forgive themselves.

The challenge is a reality that can exist from an array of offenses,
whether actual, perceived, or inappropriate. I once spoke to a precious
lady who found it difficult to forgive herself because she spent a lot of
time in her early years, sitting up through the night, worrying. Her
habit of worrying led to sleep deprivation, and this contributed to her
copious physical health problems.

The struggle to forgive self is most apparent with those who en-
tertain suicidal thoughts. These thoughts may find their "seat" in the
cognitive processes of such individuals because they form an image
of themselves as absolute failures. It is also apparent that the idea of

forgiving *oneself* may have escaped such individuals. But I wish to remind you that you are too complex, valuable, and full of potential to be an absolute failure!

If you, the reader, find yourself entertaining suicidal thoughts, even in the struggle to forgive *yourself*, I want to strongly encourage you to talk to someone who can help you with your situation. A clinical counselor will be an ideal person to contact. You may think that there is no option besides ending it all; however, if you would stop, reflect, and/or get the views and input of others, sooner or later, you can come to a viable, healthy life-preserving option.

Failure to forgive *oneself* has some antecedents. Consideration of the tremendous loss because of the offense(s) and obsessive thinking about what could have been, provide the "chair" on which failure to forgive self "sits."

Additionally, the broad and sweeping authority given to the offensive act, which is allowed to redefine an individual's personhood, is another antecedent that can lead to failure to forgive self. I spoke to this earlier and presented it as suggesting negative shame on the part of the offended, but here we note its impact on the offender as well. In the experience of negative shame, there is a lack of appreciation of *the self* that is, which is not encapsulated in the offensive act perpetrated or experienced. One who believes that their personhood is defined by an offensive act that leads to "I am no-good!" will find it difficult to forgive self. Also, individuals who believe that they deserve what they have received in negative consequences for their offenses, and nothing else, will have a great challenge with forgiving themselves.

The task before us is clear, and it entails working with such antecedents while presenting some critical considerations that can assist individuals who need to forgive themselves after they have committed an offense.

Favor for Me

While an individual may deserve to face and endure inevitable consequential repercussions, because he or she has committed an offense, there is more that they can experience! *Grace*, for instance, can be experienced. I know that grace or favor bestowed upon an individual is difficult to accept sometimes. After all, in a lot of situations, it is undeserving, and such is the case with the saving grace the Creator extends to humanity. Yet, an individual becomes the object of grace or favor when the offended decides to release them from their debt, born out of the offense(s).

Maybe, there is a need to remind persons struggling to forgive themselves that they are already recipients of a measure of the Creator's grace. If you, an offender, are alive and breathing the oxygen-rich air that is about us, you are already experiencing some dimension of the Creator's grace. Again, while the offensive act is not condoned or sanctioned by Him, you, a constituent of the physically living, are benefiting from some aspect of the Creator's favor.

So, as an offender, you are already walking in grace. You have it already! As you experience the Creator's grace, guess what? You can also experience the grace of a fellow human being, particularly one that you have offended. Therefore, it is okay to take or receive grace! You have probably been in a position already where you have given it. Somebody might have already needed and benefited from your favor, and now it is your turn to experience it. Have you heard the statement, "Hand go, hand come?" It is germane here as we ponder the receipt of grace. Because you may have to extend grace to someone in a world where offenses abound, it is all right for you to accept it!

We all need a little or much grace sometimes because of the careless, intentional, ignorant, ill-conceived, thoughtless, hasty, or inconsiderate offensive word or deed perpetrated. In our human experience, there are certain commonalities that we all share, and one of them is the need for favor. Therefore, it is not strange for me to need it, or for you to need it; moreover, it is not odd for me to receive it, or for you to receive it.

Are we not discussing forgiving ourselves in the face of an offense? So, where does the conversation on favor, needed by all, come in? It is important to note that you are no less human, a man or woman, boy or girl, as you allow the gracious release of your debt(s) by another to impact your life.

Actually, by aligning yourself with the gracious act of the offended, you can find the encouragement to release your debt also. The image of two distinguished individuals holding giant pairs of scissors, ready to cut a red ribbon for the official opening of some significant business, comes to mind. "And…on the count of three; …one…two…three," the ribbon is cut simultaneously by both individuals. So, the offended and the offender are holding their own scissors and together, they can "cut away" the debt. The lives of both are now significantly "opened for business."

The Out of Reach Past

If we could recall the past and be provided with an opportunity to say it or do it differently, the offenses and their repercussions that we know today would not be our experience. However, to recall the past into present-day reality is an impossible proposition, at least for us human beings. Therefore, it is understandable that such a reality, for some, feeds their failure to forgive themselves. Consequently, the regrets of the past, caused by the offenses perpetrated, continue to haunt some offenders' present reality.

What then do we do as we consider the offenses of the past and as we understand that we cannot alter them? How do we navigate them in our move towards forgiving ourselves? To accept the inability to change the past, as a reality, in and of itself, is a good starting place in dealing with the perpetrated grievous offenses of yesterday.

Notwithstanding the struggle in forgiving self, along with under-standing the non-trivial nature of it, acceptance can be encapsulated in the words, "It happened, and there is nothing I can do to change it!" Through such acceptance, there can be a kind of reconciliation be-tween the regrets of today and the ill-conceived behaviors of yesterday, and thus, the tension is mitigated!

Indeed, we can learn from the offenses of the past, with a view towards improving our interpersonal connections. Through the of-fenses of the past, our emotional senses can be keenly sharpened to adapt and, eventually, this can lead to a reduction in the offense(s) that occur in the relationship. In such adaptations, becoming mindful of and avoiding the offensive words and/or actions that disrupted the relationship's harmony can be viewed as a very important pursuit. In one sense, the relationship can make a turn for the better because of the adjustments made following the offense.

Learning from the past necessitates that an offender listens well! It is a process that entails perceiving and registering what the offended communicates verbally and/or non-verbally that is having an adverse effect on the relationship. Lack of regard for the offending action and its impact on the relationship will impede the "turn for the better" in the relationship. Driven by a desire for relational harmony and optimal connectivity, the ability to stay attuned to possible and actual behavioral impediments is indispensable; being a good listener is indispensable to such an ability.

Splitting Guilt and Shame

Forgiving self necessitates that we learn how to separate guilt from negative shame. Guilt can be understood as a feeling of having breached our mutual moral "oughtness." It brings us to the point where we own our offensive behavior(s). Guilt has an important job to do! It slows us down and causes us to consider our relationally upheaval words or actions with a view towards changing them. Therefore, guilt can be viewed, definitively, as a relational regulating emotion. As guilt produces conviction regarding improper behavior(s), which may lead to relationally beneficial adjustments, it can then be said that guilt is good, as a relationship building emotion.

The valuable building quality of guilt can be missed if an offender fails to own their offensive action(s). Do you know or have you heard of someone that has great difficulty in accepting blame or responsibility for the offensive conduct? They may blame others and not take an introspective look at themselves and accept their role in the offensive act or behavior. Blaming others for actions that one is responsible for is a defensive maneuver and suggests a challenge in an individual's ability to self-regulate. They also have an impaired view of selfhood. The offender's attempt to deflect blame that belongs to them may suggest that *unhealed trauma* is present in their life.

Guilt also has a regulatory function, as we bring our Creator into focus. When we offend our Creator by disobeying His behavioral codes or principles for our lives, we feel a cutting conviction, a sense of having something against us. When we experience this, the emotion of guilt is doing its job. Behavioral adjustments, in harmony with the Creator's will, should follow. So, guilt is a good thing in our human relations, as well as in our relationship with our Creator. Guilt can and needs to be appreciated!

However, guilt can become an impediment to relational health and the forgiving of *the self*. The emotion (guilt) that is good can morph into something different and have a negative impact on our lives. Too much of many things can be harmful! Too much salt, too much red meat, too much fatty foods, and too much sugar, all can have an adverse effect on our physical health. Too much guilt can have a negative impact on us psychologically and functionally!

How can we better understand too much guilt? Guilt helps us to register the inappropriate word(s) and/or action(s) so that we make the necessary adjustments/adaptations in the relationship. This results in an enhanced relational connectedness. Thus, it can be said that guilt came at the right time, did its job, and then left. However, if guilt lingers long after the conviction, the release of debt, or the adjustment, it has probably changed into the emotion of negative shame. Remember, this can be experienced through the offensive act(s) being given the leeway to redefine the offender altogether. According to Blake M. Riek, in experiencing such shame, the offender has a "global evaluation"[8] of self.

Consequently, their view of *the self* may become false in, "I am no-good!" which signals that the individual has experienced too much guilt. It can be easily understood then, given this perspective, why it is so difficult to forgive self. But we must also remember that the offense(s) is not the person that offends, and that the offense perpetrated can never encapsulate the personhood of such an individual.

Therefore, understanding how guilt can morph into negative shame, it is incumbent, within this process of forgiving self that the offender separate the two emotions. This is accomplished by letting guilt do its work and appreciating such a work but not allowing it to persist to the point where it negatively redefines our person. We can check or control guilt, especially since it can serve as a relationship builder!

Cognitively separating guilt and negative shame is one thing, but what do we do with the negative emotion after separation? It is here, that we again call on our old friend, emotional substitution. Its action ensures that the feeling of "I am no-good!" is replaced with one that affirms, "I made a mistake, but it is not who I am," or "I still have some good qualities." When negative shame is supplanted with such affirming emotions, it becomes much easier to forgive self for the offensive action(s) perpetrated in the past.

I Am Still Lovable

In our interpersonal relationships, one of the things that draw human beings to one another is affection or love. Indeed, "It feels so good to love somebody and somebody loves you back," as one of the popular songs suggests. This reciprocity of love is valued in the relationship shared between husband and wife, parents and their children, and between good friends.

However, when an offense is perpetrated, the "cable of love" that connects us is strained and sometimes broken. Notwithstanding that genuine love should find traction and fulfillment in times of relational strain and offense, sometimes love morphs and offending individuals become the object of hate (I hasten to remind us that such a deposition is not congruent with the Creator's design for our lives).

The offense occurs and subsequently the relationship sometimes changes and, as was noted, things may never be the same again. The offender, who once was the object of shared joy, purpose, and pursuit, now becomes the object of suspicions, scorn, and neglect. It is such consequences brought on by an offense that can lead to the offender asking the question, "Am I lovable?"

Even with offenses against the Creator, the offender, when weighed down with feelings of failure, could develop a view and sense of *the self* that says, "I am too far gone" or "He does not want anything to do with me." These all point to the perspective that one is beyond the love of the Creator. Such a perspective is far from the truth regarding the

Creator's disposition towards His offenders. Here, we note that Scripture clarifies the attitude our Creator has towards His offenders: "But God demonstrates His own love toward us, in that while we were yet sinners [*offenders*], Christ died for us" (Romans 5:8).

The above verse provides for us the temperament of our Creator, which is one of affection towards us as human beings. The verse also reveals the kind of love that He extends towards humankind. It is a love that is demonstrative and not merely couched in the profundity of intentional words. Do you know of those who only talk about love without corresponding deeds?

I knew a man who resolutely pledged his commitment to his girl-friend when her health was relatively good; however, when her health had deteriorated, he was nowhere to be found. He seemed to have forgotten the pledge he had made to her. In my country, we would say, "Bush crack and man gone!" Which is a colloquialism that suggests that when the "heat is on" there is an abandonment of one's former position. This is not the kind of behavior the Creator demonstrates when He says that He loves us. Such an expressed love is one that is still extended to mankind even though their debts, as offenders, have not been removed. This tells me that past and present offenders are not out of the scope and reach of the Creator's love; they are still able to receive His love and forgiveness.

Indeed, despite their grievous, offensive actions, offenders are still lovable! Their offenses do not prevent them from becoming the objects of the Creator's love. Without a doubt though, such a love must be experienced, and offenders must continue in it for it to find fulfillment in their lives. Yet, it remains extended to them even if they reject it!

While the offender can be assured of the Creator's love, post the offense, they can also experience love from their fellow human beings. Here, I want to remind you that we as human beings can share in the same relationship building qualities that we see in the Creator. As He loves, so can we, and as He releases from debt, so can we!

I know a man who married a woman who had two children out of wedlock from a prior relationship. Yet, because of his love for the woman, he married her and continues to love her. Indeed, this was a noble deed. It underscores that, not only do we have the capacity to love, but also, in spite of our offenses, we can still become the objects of human love. The offenders are still lovable!

The struggle to forgive ourselves is made easier, as we consider how, from the perspective of the Creator (which is the ultimate perspective that really matters), we who are offenders, can still be loved and receive love. Moreover, this "lovableness" is further revealed in our ability to love one another, beyond our offensive behaviors.

Intact Value Ensures Fulfillment of Purpose

Critically linked to being lovable is the value that offenders possess in *the self*. Actually, because of their value, they remain lovable. Offenders need to realize that their worth was not obliterated because of their offensive conduct.

However, no matter how lovable offenders are, forgiving self may need to begin with them taking an inventory of *the self*, as it currently exists. Most likely, this assessment would reveal intact positive traits. Perhaps, thoughtfulness would still be in place after the offensive behavior. There may also be a warm friendly smile, an encouraging disposition, an attitude of persistence, a special ability like being an excellent organizer, or one who has an exemplary work ethic. What positive traits do you see in yourself as you do the assessment? As the assessment reveals positive qualities still attached to *the self*, it also reveals an offender's worth or value.

Because offenders' worth is intact, post offense(s), their purpose can still be fulfilled. Offenders can walk on towards and in the perceived reason for existence. This includes the Creator's purpose for their life, individual purpose, as well as purpose towards their fellow human beings. Actually, all can be summed up in the Creator's purpose for the individual's life. So, the offender's offensive behavior(s) need not prevent them from fulfilling their purpose. To put it another way, the offensive action(s) is not tantamount with failure to fulfill one's purpose.

Offenders who realize their inherent value can also forgive themselves and proceed towards fulfilling their purpose in the human experience. Moreover, with the knowledge of value being intact, their sense of self-worth can be strengthened even though offenses were per-petrated. As they move towards a healthy state spiritually, cognitively, physically, emotionally, and socially through acceptance of their inher-ent value, there can be a renewed sense of self-worth and self-hood. Post offenses, these are very important for offenders, as they would navigate their interpersonal relationships in their personal attributes.

Offenders who struggle to forgive themselves should understand that their dignity could be restored. Individuals sullied by the offensive actions they perpetrated can once again be respected, as they shine through the fulfillment of their purpose. Yes, relational healing may not occur right away, but it can happen, just give it some time! Even-tually, people will accord us the very thing that they expect from others – respect and dignity. If we can't get them from one individual, all is not lost because we can get them from others.

In sum, we can be motivated to forgive *the self* because of our in-herent value, which transcends the offense(s) and enables us to func-tion in our purpose.

Boundaries for Inappropriate Blame

Let us take another excursion! This one will be brief! I hope you are still buckled up! You have a wonderful neighbor who allows you to borrow his lawn mower to mow your overgrown lawn; for this, you are more than grateful, especially since yours is being repaired. Your neighbor also has a nice, happy, little Chow dog. However, he has a life endangering habit of running out of your neighbor's yard into the busy street. You noticed that a few times when he ran out into the street, he was almost crushed by passing vehicles.

Being concerned about your kind neighbor's pet, you informed him about the precarious situation his dog periodically finds himself in, as he allows him to run into the street. However, your neighbor seems not to be bothered by his dog's behavior.

You persist further and try to explain to your neighbor that you fear something terrible is going to happen to the happy dog if it is not constrained. However, your neighbor remains apathetic about the situation. So, you continue to observe this nice dog running out of your neighbor's yard, placing itself in harm's way.

While the above story provides a scenario between two neighbors and a dog, it also sheds light on the subject of responsibility. In observing your neighbor's dog, you probably would want to take on the task of restraining it yourself to prevent it from dashing out into the dangerous street. However, you do not because you also realize that if there was any restraining to do, it squarely resides in the purview of your neighbor, who owns the dog – the dog is your neighbor's responsibility! You do not want anything bad to happen to that nice dog, but if it did, it would be all on your neighbor, especially since you brought the dog's behavior to his attention.

Sometimes when there is a difficulty in forgiving self, responsibility is misappropriated. In such cases, individuals can be said to function from an Omni-powerful or all-powerful perspective, where they see themselves as causing and owning everything. Surely, this is not the case!

I know that, in some cases, when individuals take on responsibilities that do not belong to them, care must be exercised to help them to set the appropriate boundaries. In this process, misappropriated responsibility is relinquished and placed where it belongs. This is of particular importance when we consider the young tender ones (our children), who are violated by unprincipled adults, and who develop the tendency to think that they caused the negative behavior that such adults perpetrated against them. The truth is that they did not; they are innocent.

And so, we have situations where guilt is misapplied, which not only leads to misapplied ownership of the offending action or word, but also results in an unfounded struggle to forgive self. How do we then place the blame/responsibility where it belongs? We can start the reassignment of responsibility by looking at the misapplied guilt, which is a primary issue here.

So, in the cases of individuals who have experienced groundless struggle to forgive themselves, there need to be a release of the inappropriate guilt. In keeping with the limited scope of this work, maybe a few introspective questions would help to dislodge such guilt: Was

I a child when the deed was done to me? In my naivety was the other person seductive in their words and behavior? If the answer to the two questions above is a definitive "Yes," then we are pointing to a state of your innocence in the matter. Similarly, there are other questions that can be asked: Could I have controlled the actions and decisions of the other person? Did I speak the word? Did I commit the deed? If the answer is "No," we are still in a state of innocence regarding the negative situation.

Individuals who experience a foundationless challenge in forgiving themselves also need to be able to place blame at the "door" of the persons to whom it belongs. You might not have seen the individual, who perpetrated the offense, in years or they might have died. So, reassigning the blame to their address will prove to be challenging, but you can still do it. In such cases, there are a few exercises that can help you with this blame reassignment. Writing a letter, to explain to the person who may be long gone that you are not responsible for their actions, can be an effective exercise in reassigning the blame after you realize you are innocent in the matter. After writing the letter, you can shred or burn it. This process will help you to re-contextualize the offense and bring closure while leaving the responsibility at the "door" of the one who committed the offense.

Another approach is more creative as it involves an empty chair. In this exercise, you would see or visualize in the chair the person whose responsibility you have been carrying around with you all these years. The next step is to speak to the person as if they were actually there, occupying the chair. Tell them how you feel about the wrong that they have perpetrated against you and how it was inappropriate for you to have been holding yourself responsible for their improprieties. Also, tell the person that you will no longer be carrying around the blame that belongs to them.

For the actual perpetrators that are still accessible, notwithstanding your safety, an audience with them may be advisable. Courage is critical here! Courage is needed to tell them how they have negatively impacted your life. Courage is needed to let them know that you have been blaming yourself for their offensive conduct. Courage is also needed to tell them that you will no longer carry around the burden of their responsibility, and that you release it over to them for you have been carrying it long enough. You can muster up the necessary courage to do it! You may want to take a friend along to help bolster your courage in this very important exercise of responsibility reassignment.

Patience, Compassion and Empathy Towards the Self

I once told a family member that she needed to be more patient with herself. The person was perplexed about that bit of advice, so she asked, "What do you mean, be more patient with myself?" We may know what it means to be patient with others by giving them the benefit of the doubt, understanding their missteps, and encouraging them to engage in appropriate behaviors, and so forth.

However, tolerating *the self* is also a viable and necessary proposition for our consideration. Giving oneself the leeway to adjust, expand, and learn from mistakes are all important aspects of being patient with one's person, which is essential to forgiving self.

Do you remember the process of acquiring a new skill? Perhaps, you were learning how to ride a bicycle or drive a manual transmission vehicle for the first time. Or, can you recall being trained for some new post at work, under the watchful eyes of an instructor? Whatever the experience, what was your disposition while learning?

I surmise that you realized it was not an instant process, and you gave yourself room to make mistakes, as your instructor did. You expected to "grind a few gears" in starting to work the manual transmission vehicle. You were patient with yourself while you learned the new skill.

Acquiring the skill of living is an ongoing process. We are constantly encountering new experiences and learning from them in our time on earth. Whether young or old, accomplished or just setting out on a career path, we are always in a learning mode. Because this is the case, mistakes and missteps are concomitant with such a mode. Therefore, we need to be patient with ourselves, as we remain under the tutelage of life.

As indicated above, patience with *the self* is critically linked to forgiving oneself. If your view of self is regimented and excludes the possibility of missteps, or inaccurate judgments, or poor decisions, then you may be too critical of your person. This regimented view can lead to protracted guilt and to the encaging emotion of failing to forgive self. Again, I am not excusing inappropriate behavior, I am just pointing out that if healing and emotional liberation, in forgiving self, is going to take place, patience towards *the self* is an imperative.

Even the Creator, understandably, gives His people room to navigate through the vexing offensive issues related to healing:

Therefore, strengthen the hands that are weak and the knees that are feeble, and make straight paths for your feet, so that the limb which is lame may not be put out of joint, but rather be healed (Hebrews 12:12-13).

Offenses against the Creator are not condoned here, and neither are His people encouraged to be content with the offending weak and feeble areas that may be a part of their lives; however, I believe that the Creator is patient towards them in their move towards healing.

Therefore, the question directed towards us, as human beings, could be, "Should we not be patient with ourselves?" So, you have this three-pronged tension of understanding the ideal, misstep, and move in the direction of healing. It is a tension undergirded by patience, including patience towards *the self.*

As there is sometimes very little struggle to be patient with others, being compassionate towards our fellow human beings may also not be much of a challenge, at least for some of us. But I ask, "What about being compassionate towards yourself, even though you acted in an offensive way?"

Having compassion for oneself takes into consideration the context of an offense. The offending word said, or deed done might have been perpetrated out of ignorance. Is this not a fitting situation to have compassion for oneself: That is, when we speak or act in an offensive way because of the absence of and/or presence of limited knowledge? If you had the "full scoop" on the situation, you know that things would have been different. Nevertheless, the offense occurred!

Yet, compassion for oneself is not restricted to the offense that was carried out within a context of ignorance. It can find traction, even in circumstances where the offense was perpetrated with the full knowledge of the offender. It is quite possible that he or she was cognizant of the fact that someone was going to get hurt and be relationally impeded or disabled by the offensive action or word. However, compassion towards *the self* is still viable and necessary, especially when there is remorse and regret for what was said or done, and the offender is experiencing the consequences of the offense perpetrated.

I hasten, again, to remind the reader that offenses against the Creator (Scripture delineate these) are not sanctioned; therefore, concerted effort ought to be made to avoid such. However, when they do occur, the offense(s), perpetrated and regretted, provides an opportunity for learning and adjustment. It is in this pattern of knowledgeable offense, regret, learning, and adjustment that compassion becomes necessary and finds good traction for forgiving self.

Like patience towards self, compassion towards self helps to "pave the way" that is "unpaved" and difficult to navigate in the work of forgiving self. Notice, that I have also referred to the process of forgiving self as a work; this is because focused effort and energy must be brought to it, notwithstanding the difficulties that may be associated with it.

Finally, in forgiving oneself, the role of empathy must be brought into focus. You probably have no problem exhibiting a participatory understanding of the feelings of another. You can understand their hurt, anger, frustrations, disappointments, sadness, regrets, and even their joy. What about being aware of and engaging or sharing in your feelings after your offensive behavior? You can get to that point by looking objectively at your circumstances, station in life, or by having a broadened perspective of the context of your offense. It may be, that as you consider the circumstances that led to your offensive behavior, you could easily identify the thing that was lacking in your developmental environment – if it were there, things would have been a whole lot different.

Perhaps, your parents allowed you to have your way "all the time" and "never" denied you anything through a limiting "No!" You now understand that if you had been more exposed to the "No!" that boundaries afford then you probably would have respected them more in others and not offend your fellow human beings. Nevertheless, you can now see that, in your developmental environment, the lack of disciplinary structures contributed to your offensive behavior.

Still, your developmental environment might have had something added that you should not have been exposed to, such as protracted sexual abuse by some unprincipled adult who should have known better. And because of this abuse you were exposed to a world you were not supposed to encounter because of your tenderness, lack of maturity, poor judgment, and ill preparedness. In being ensnared by this world, because of the perpetual abuse, certain sexual behaviors became the norm and they laid the foundation for committing various ill-judged offenses. In your case, you may be able to say, "Sexual impropriety gave rise to sexual impropriety!"

Now, at your current station in life, you have acknowledged your improprieties and have turned away from them; yet, the struggle to forgive yourself persists because of the guilt associated with such behaviors.

Here, there is a need to revisit the genesis of the abuse. Recall your innocence in the matter as that adult violated you and took away the thing that was sacred to you. At the same time, they destabilized and confused you about the reality, proper context, and moral "oughtness" of the sexual experience, at such a tender age.

While in your tender state, it all began with an offense against you; your offensive behavior was birth out of the exploitation(s) of another. Consider how tender you were, and as you reflect, know that you can have empathy towards *tender you.*

Moreover, as you reflect on the genesis of your offensive behavior, while recognizing *tender you*, you are re-contextualizing it through a much broader view. You know I am not suggesting that the wrong that was perpetrated by you is excused; rather, because your view is expanded to include the beginning of it all, you are better positioned to release yourself from the debt or guilt of your offensive behavior, in the here and now.

Again, it is very important to understand that, despite your offensive behavior, your value is still intact. You too, as the offender, must remember that the improper action does not sum you up as a person. No, not at all! Your worth persists beyond your offense(s) and so does your potential!

We have looked at some key areas in our move towards forgiving self. Offenders, including those who struggle to forgive themselves out of misappropriated guilt, can work effectively towards releasing themselves from their offensive debts, even if they are wrongly applied. The receipt of grace, accepting the unalterable past, separating guilt from negative shame, being assured of one's "lovableness" and value, along with the ability to place blame where it belongs, while being patient, compassionate, and empathetic towards *the self*, are all critical considerations for extending forgiveness to self.

For further deliberation…

1. Emotional healing can become a goal for the offended after an offense. Should it also become a goal for the offender?

2. What advice would you give those who may think that their lives are an absolute failure after carrying out offenses?

3. How would you reconcile not being able to change the past and learning from it with regard to offenses?

4. Guilt is described as an emotion that regulates relationships. Do you agree? Why or why not?

5. How is it that, after an egregious offense, the offender can get up and still fulfill their purpose and potential?

6. Courage is needed to reassign responsibility. But is it needed to forgive self?

7. The idea of looking at *the self* as the object of patience, compassion, and empathy may take some getting used to after committing offense(s). Is there any progress to forgive oneself without it?

Chapter Nine

Other Considerations in Extending Forgiveness...

Modeling Forgiveness

Forgiving an offender has far-reaching effects! As human beings, we are constantly exemplars of what we say and do. Others are watching to learn from and mimic us (especially the children) and be guided through life. Do not think for one second that you are not being observed in what you say and do! While we know that wrong behavior can be learned and mimicked; yet, there are positive things that can be passed on to others. One such positive thing is the act of extending forgiveness.

A wife can become a good example to her husband when it comes to forgiving his offenses. The employee, who has been offended, can become a good example to an offending employer. Parents, offended by children, can be good examples to them, as they release them from their debt(s). And, even the rude neighbor, who keeps blowing his leaves onto your property, can be provided with a noble model of how to extend forgiveness for this offensive act.

In our world, we are provided with negative after negative examples of what it means to be unforgiving – its fruit is ubiquitous by its very nature. From the horrendous instances of road rage to one nation that continues to flex its military might because of past conflicts (e.g., North Korea's stance against South Korea), we see the profile and consequences of unforgiveness. Extending forgiveness refreshingly provides an alternative to this negative norm. At the same time, it lays down a pattern for behavioral adoption that fosters healing and optimization of our human relationships and experiences.

When we extend forgiveness to others, our world becomes a better place. Think about what drives the negative actions of terrorists. Unforgiveness is brought into sharp focus as part of what forms the foundation for their diabolical plots. Extending forgiveness not only can halt the vicious cycle of offenses that they perpetrate, but it can help them and us to demonstrate why we are different from the dogs that attack and devour one another. There is something different about us that distinguish us from the animals. It is clear that we are made in the image of our Creator, and our ability to forgive one another is a part of this difference.

Human accomplishments are great! From our trip to the moon to putting communication at our fingertips with the latest technological devices such as smart phones, man shines in his creativity like his Creator. Extending forgiveness not only affords us the opportunity to become positive examples, but it further provides for us the option to demonstrate our greatness, uniqueness, and creativity, as we deal with the problems and challenges that come along with our interpersonal relationships.

Inspiration from Others

While we can model what it is to extend forgiveness, others can also inspire us in this noble experience. If we look carefully, we can identify individuals around us who have wrestled with unforgiveness but no longer do because they have successfully released the offender from their debt(s) that came along with the offense(s). I believe one such individual is Hillary Clinton, who was one of the US presidential candidates in 2016. More than a decade earlier, and before the presidential campaign, her husband, former President Bill Clinton, while president of the United States, found himself in a compromising inappropriate relationship with one of his work associates. However, based on the couple's public image, some markers indicate Hillary Clinton released her husband from the debt that he had incurred due to this offensive behavior.

One marker was Hillary's decision not to divorce her husband, notwithstanding his improprieties. Another marker was seen in Bill Clinton's support of Hillary Clinton in her bid for the White House.

He spoke in a very profound way at the Democratic National Party's convention of her, providing reasons why he believed that she would make a good president of the United States. At the same time, in my estimation, he also provided reasons for his endearment towards her.

Still, another marker was that their public relationship seemed to be characterized by relational harmony, despite the offenses of the past. Therefore, it is not a far-fetched conclusion that she had forgiven her husband. In this vein, she has become an inspiration, a model of encouragement for others who struggle to extend forgiveness.

Not only does Hillary Clinton occupy this position regarding the process of extending forgiveness, but also another wife, whom we will call Pat. The discovery of a child's photo in her husband's wallet confirmed Pat's suspicions – her husband had breached their marital covenant and fathered a child outside of their marriage. Pat was, understandably, "mad" about it, particularly given the other woman's bold and brazen demands on her husband. She was also angry because she felt that she could have fulfilled, as a woman, all that her husband needed.

Over a decade had gone by since the offensive action of her husband. Although Pat acknowledged that the situation did not bother her as it used to, she admitted that "It was hard in the beginning!" Pat was asked about what brought her to the state where the situation did not bother her, as it did when the offense first came to light. She indicated three things: 1) the regret that her husband expressed about his actions; 2) his fight to keep their marriage when he learned that divorce was considered; and, 3) his behavioral change that demonstrated his renewed commitment to Pat and the marriage. All worked together to help her release her husband from his debt. Pat even acknowledged that trust had been restored in their relationship, but she was now more vigilant in the marriage since she had been "burned" before.

Pat serves as an inspirational model of encouragement in this process of extending forgiveness to others who have wronged us. The struggle was real for her, but she overcame it by being empathetic towards her husband. We have looked at Hillary Clinton and Pat and have found contemporary examples in them that can inspire us to release our debtors. Can you think of any other examples?

In presenting our two examples, I noticed that they shared something in common other than extending forgiveness to their husbands. Did you notice it? It was the relational harmony that they shared with their husbands more than a decade after the offenses.

The passing of time must be commended for its part in the emotional healing that needs to take place after an offense. However, I want also to point out that relational harmony need not take a decade to be achieved between the offended and offender. With respect to our context of offenses and the accompaniments associated with extending forgiveness, relational harmony can be attained in a short time.

A Forgiving Lifestyle

Lifestyle is an interesting word. It speaks to the way a person lives. Certain lifestyles leave much to be desired; others lift a standard of nobility that is worth emulating. Lifestyles are impacted by our behavioral patterns – as goes my behavior, so goes my lifestyle. However, both behavior and lifestyle need not be left to arbitrary influences in life, for an individual can determine their behavior and lifestyle. Choice features prominently in both instances. As conscientious, decision-making beings, we choose our behavior and lifestyle.

Extending forgiveness can become an integral part of our behavior and lifestyle as we choose to incorporate it into our interpersonal relationships. The certainty of offenses, their cyclical and intermittent nature, along with our expectations of them (offenses are not condoned here), necessitates a response that allows for coping with and enduring them. Such a response is found in a lifestyle characterized by the tendency to extend forgiveness to others.

It is suggested here that the regularity and inevitability of offenses can co-exist with a lifestyle that is accustomed to extending forgiveness to others.

Universalize It!

If you are seeking to forgive your offender, notwithstanding the challenge that you may currently have with their offense, there is a high probability that you have been at this particular juncture of your life before. You might have had the opportunity and the experience of releasing someone from their debt and offense associated with it in the past. The experience, therefore, is not foreign to you; you know what it means not to concern yourself with an offense.

Because you have extended forgiveness before, there were some principles that worked in your life in the past to help you release your debtor from their debt. The principle of love might have been in place or the principle of empathy or the principle of mercy. These might have worked together and brought you to the point of release. So, you have the experience of release! Additionally, you also have the resources within you to help you forgive an offender who may have perpetrated a more challenging offense against you.

The key to understanding this is being able to identify and acknowledge such resources. Objectively, as you look at your person, you may conclude that you are a lover of people, in a demonstrative way; able to share in the feelings of another; and, have a "bag" of mercy that you can open, retrieve some mercy, and mete out. These resources are within you because you accessed them before. The task then is to spread them throughout your interpersonal connections. You can "universalize" such resources; just as they were deployed in the case of one of your debtors, they can be deployed in the case of another. You can spread them towards your current offender, who offended you in a most egregious way.

Relationship Retention

Relationships are sustained by extending forgiveness. Think about what might be at stake in a relationship due to an offense, particularly, if it results in unforgiveness by the offended. This negative emotion can help to topple all that has been good in our interpersonal relationships.

For a husband and wife, at risk is the many years together, characterized by mutual interests, investing in each other, and accomplishing much together for themselves and their family. High stakes are also seen in an employee and employer's relationship that may be characterized by many years of mutually beneficial rewards in a business that has sustained both parties.

Then there are the ever-changing positive relational dynamics that may be attached to parent/child relationships – from the parents' support and care that is extended to the child to the support and care that the child continues to give their parents.

Through the years, you have treasured the valuable friendship that you share with your best friend from high school. You cannot believe that it has been thirty years since you have been friends!

With objective eyes, you can see the beauty of the relationship before the offense occurred. Run the entire length and breadth of human relations, and one would find that there is value attached to our interpersonal connectedness. I believe that you can appreciate that unforgiveness threatens and reduces the retention of such value in relationships. Like a rifle that is used to shoot a goose down out of a valuable formation with other geese flying through the airspaces, so it is that unforgiveness can ruin the mutually beneficial dynamics found in a relationship; it can "shoot it down!"

Extending forgiveness can set a relationship back on course, where it again becomes mutually beneficial for all parties concerned, even though it may lose formation due to an offense.

The Possibility of Greater Love

Biblical Scripture, in Luke chapter seven, reveals the story of a woman who was involved in loose or immoral living; she probably was a prostitute. However, her encounter with Jesus, while He was having dinner, manifested something unusual – with her tears, she incessantly wet Jesus' feet and wiped them with her hair. Additionally, she anointed His feet with perfume.

The dinner host of Jesus took issue with His permitting the immoral woman to do what she did, so he said to himself, "'...If this man were a prophet, He would know who and what sort of person this woman is who is touching Him, that she is a sinner'" (Luke 7:39). This statement of the host, spoken to himself, invoked a direct and open set of teachings on forgiveness by Jesus.

As Jesus taught, He brought focus to a moneylender who had two debtors; one owed him a large sum of money and the other, not so large. When both were not able to pay their debt, the moneylender graciously forgave them both.

Out of this story, Jesus asked the host which one of the debtors will love the moneylender more; was it the one forgiven of the large debt or the one forgiven of the not so substantial debt? You probably know the answer of the host, who answered correctly: The one forgiven of the larger debt would love more. Jesus applied this correct answer to the woman's situation because her debt, which was great before her Creator, was forgiven. Therefore, she loved more, as evident in her tears, the wiping of Jesus' feet with her hair and her anointing them with perfume.

Do you see where I am going with this story? From the above Scripture, we can understand, there is the possibility of a debtor, who has been forgiven much (those forgiven of lesser debt can find themselves in this category of individuals also), demonstrating gratitude to the offended that has released their debt. And this comes about due to the great love the offender may exhibit towards the offended.

We can certainly say that such a display of love occurs out of a sense of indebtedness. Repayment is out of the question, but this does not cancel out a sense of appropriate indebtedness for the grace received, following the release of the debt(s). This is especially the case when we consider the extent of the forgiveness of our debts by the Creator.

Please do not misunderstand me! I am in no way advocating that extending forgiveness to a debtor should merely be motivated out of what the offended receives, namely, a display of great love by the offender (whatever that may look like).

My goal here is to point out that when releasing our debtors from their debts, we possibly position ourselves to be the objects of great love (manifested in both unusual and usual ways) cultivated in and emanating from a spirit of gratitude in offenders. I believe that this understanding does not make it difficult for the offended to release the offender from their debts; instead, it makes it easier.

However, other motivators lead to the release of an offender's debt. I believe you know some of them by now, which include, the wellbeing (psychological, physical, social, spiritual, etc.) of the offended; relational growth in the offender; and, preserving of the value of the interpersonal relationship that is threatened by the offense, just to name a few.

It is good to know that there are factors that can motivate individuals to extend forgiveness. This work seeks to provide an understanding of such factors. The offender's gratitude, demonstrated by their great love towards the offended, is one of these motivating factors.

Re-buildable Trust

There is need for us to speak further about trust concerning this matter of extending forgiveness. As you know, an offense has the potential to interrupt the trust that exists in our interpersonal relationships — the offender functions in a way that does not safeguard the interest(s) of the offended.

The breach of trust results in, among other emotional wounds, hurt, which can further disrupt the harmony that exists in a relationship. After striving for and experiencing intimacy, through risk-taking and becoming vulnerable, the pain that results from the violation of trust is understandable. However, trust has a certain resiliency attached to it; its nature is such that it can be rebuilt, even in the face of injury caused by an offense. The offended can once again be assured that the offender will look after their interests. It can be restored – trust can bounce back! But its restoration is a process. Aided by the offender's change of behavior, and resolve to build again in their commitment to the relationship, trust restoration finds significant traction.

This is beautifully seen in a wife's realignment with her husband, and through her commitment to work with and support him, along with her determination to remain by his side, even after his habitual "womanizing" ways! In an actual case, the offended wife's ability to trust her husband again "paved" the way for the value of their relationship to be showcased and seen in her role as caregiver, right up to his demise. It was a role that she took great delight in, although it was challenging at times.

Of course, a number of factors might have worked together to cause the wife's resilient trust to be restored in the above situation. Maybe, it was her dogged determination to make the marriage work because she took her vows seriously. Or, it could have been her unconditional love for her husband. Or maybe, it was her Christian values that found their practical expressions, as they impacted her husband's life, and as she decided to "move" them from the "corridors" of knowledge, understanding, words, and intentions. Because of my association with the wife, I believe that such values helped to make it possible for trust to be restored in the relationship with her husband. Whatever the cause, before death did them part, there was a clear display of a marital relationship, operating in the ideal, undergirded by trust.

In the above account, the wife's example of trust restored had some fundamental pillars attached to it. Because restoration of trust is a process, it is very important to mention that the decision to trust again, which stems from our volition or the exercise of our free will, plays a critical role in the experience. The wife had to decide, once more, to allow her husband to look out for her interests, as they moved their relationship forward. While impacted by changes in the husband's behavior, the restoration of trust in their relationship was predicated on the wife's decision to trust again.

Another pillar in the process of the restoration of trust is patience. The farmer plants the seeds of his crop, but he needs patience if he wants to see the fruit of those seeds. Likewise, the offended needs patience if he or she is to see the evidence of trust on the rebuilding path – they cannot rush it!

This patience or forbearance has a couple of objects, which include: the offender, in their adaptive self and effort to be different; and, the offended, as they navigate the restoration of trust experienced with its emotional flux. Perhaps, as the offended, you have not been in a conscientious trust rebuilding exercise before and/or the experience is new to you – patience is needed! The wife, in the above story, had to be patient with her repentant husband and herself as they worked together to restore their trust in each other!

Still, another essential pillar that leads to the restoration of trust is risk-taking. "Why does the image of a small turtle crossing a busy street keep entering my mind at this juncture of this work?" Can you see the turtle taking the risk in crossing the street? In order for it to enjoy the gains on the other side of the street, it has to take the risk!

When one has been "burned" before, that is, emotionally, it is understandable that such experiences result in the construction of defense barriers around our inner emotions and self. The "burn" can also result in fear of venturing out, relationally, with *the self*. Consequently, relationships are not developed based on their authentic footing. This posture, however, is not in harmony with the process of rebuilding trust. An individual must take the risk in order to reap the reward; the offended must responsibly venture out, again, with *the self* that is (the true/actual self).

The wife, in our story, had to lower her emotional defenses and venture out with *the self* that is (her true self) to experience restored trust. She had to become vulnerable again! She had to uncover core or inner dimensions of herself before her husband in order to share in the kind of intimacy that restored trust affords.

I noted earlier that the rebuilding of trust is a process. It is a process that finds traction through the behavioral changes in the offender, and it "paves" the way for the recapture of the ideal, a harmonious relationship. It can be said that extending forgiveness is the harbinger of rebuilding trust! Releasing the offender from their debt, which accompanied the offense, gives clearance for the process of trust restoration to begin.

As you can see, there are several considerations that impact the extending of forgiveness to an offender, and this work has sought to reveal some of them. Also, in extending forgiveness, there are a number of consequential implications that affect our interpersonal relationships. While this chapter has not dealt exhaustively with such implications, I believe it has revealed how far-reaching the process of extending forgiveness can go in our lives.

For further deliberation…

1. Why might an individual be interested in modeling how best to extend forgiveness to an offender?

2. What benefit is there in identifying those who have been offended and have managed to forgive their offenders?

3. Do you really think that you have the resources within you to extend forgiveness to your offender? Why or why not?

4. Should those offended be concerned about the benefits that extending forgiveness has to offer them?

5. There are several factors that impact the restoration of trust when it has been violated because of an offense in the relationship. Do you think that risk-taking by the offended is an indispensible factor? Why or why not?

I Forgive

Chapter Ten

Recalibrating Forgiveness

The struggle to forgive an offender of their debt(s) can exist before the release occurs in the pre-forgiven state. There can also persist a struggle for the offended to hold on to such a release once it occurs. The offense was forgiven, but there still occurs, in the offended, feelings that seek to hold the offender in a pre-forgiven state. That is, in a state of unforgiveness. Consequently, there may also persist intermittent feelings that insist that the offender be held "accountable" or made to pay for the damage done and/or the loss experienced. Still, there may even be an urge to respond in kind. I believe you know the spirit of "Tit for tat, you kill my dog, I kill your cat." There may also exist the struggle to view the offender as whole again. He or she may even be despised.

Moreover, a feeling of superiority may also form towards the offender who was forgiven: "Because you messed up, you can never be at my level again in this relationship." And so, the struggle to keep the offender forgiven can persist! Several factors contribute to this persistency. Because of our brain's biological function, and its ability to create memory patterns to help us adapt for survival purposes, there can be an automatic recall of the offensive event. Hurtful feelings can also arise, as we become more conscious of the injury experienced triggered by a scent, a scene, a word, or a certain similar context in which the offense occurred.

Some of these memory patterns, especially severely traumatic ones, can be quite obsessive in nature, where, for example, an individual may find it quite difficult to stop thinking about certain aspects of an offense that was committed against them. The intrusive nature of the offensive thoughts keeps the offense emotionally fresh, and the struggle to keep the forgiven, forgiven, persists.

Further, the memory of the event can remain at the fore of our consciousness because of our imagination and speculations regarding the offense. This is especially true in cases involving sexual offenses. The absence of "all" of the details surrounding such offenses can drive the offended to fill in the gaps imaginatively. In doing so, however, not only can an individual be creating a false reality, but he or she may perpetuate the hurt in the offense. And as the hurt of the offense is perpetuated, so is the struggle to keep the forgiven, forgiven.

The behavior of the forgiven can also cause there to be a struggle within the offended regarding keeping the offender released from their debt. An offender may be in a state of flux in relation to their offensive behavior. They want to do right, as dictated by our mutual moral "oughtness"; however, inconsistencies arise in the effort being made. The offender might have made some significant strides, since being forgiven, to avoid the offending behavior, yet, the offense may reoccur, or they may commit some other offense.

The reoccurring offensive pattern can bring with it a challenge for the offended to keep the forgiven, forgiven. Sometimes a message may accompany such a pattern. As false as it may be! As it may suggest to the offended that the offender was not repentant or sorry for their offensive behavior, or it may convey that they never intended to do any better. One can then see how the offender's behavioral flux and the message it may bring could perpetuate the hurt that the offensive action produced in the offended, and, thus, increase the struggle to keep release in place for the individual forgiven.

For the offended, memory patterns of the offense, imagination, and behavioral inconsistencies in the offender can all cause to exist the struggle to keep the forgiven in a state characterized by the release of the debt. Offenders can also experience such a struggle. Although the offended have forgiven them and they have managed to forgive themselves, yet for the offenders, maintaining such a release can prove problematic, especially because of the memory of the offensive behavior, the constant encounter with the offended, and the shame associated with the offense.

Not only can memory patterns in the brain of the offended, produced by the offense, be one of the causes for the struggle to keep the forgiven, forgiven. But such patterns can be the basis for offenders being challenged with holding the release of debt towards *the self* in place.

The offender's ability to naturally recall the offense can be just as problematic as the offended ability to do the same. With both parties, recalling the offensive behavior can bring with it feelings of hurt and self-disappointment that works to cancel out the release of the debt.

Seeing someone, who was offended on a perpetual basis, can keep the regretful and shameful feelings associated with the offense alive for the offender. But if the offended remains out of sight, the guilty feelings produced by the offense can easily be kept out of the conscious mind of the offender. However, such invisibility or distance is not always possible – an employee, offended by a fellow employee, who must work with them at the same establishment, is a case in point.

The opposite, then, may occur for the offender who is not only experiencing regret and feelings of shame but who is close to the offended. Specifically, with the offended in sight, the feelings of guilt persist as the memories fill the mind. Perpetual regretful shameful feelings, therefore, makes it difficult, in such instances, for offenders to hold on to *the forgiven self*.

Another consideration is that of negative shame. We have already seen how impeding such shame can be towards emotional healing. However, its impact on the life of an offender is not singular or one-time in nature; sometimes, it can have multiple or rippling effects on the offender. And, just as there is a struggle to retain the release of a debt towards *the self*, there can also be a struggle to keep negative shame at bay.

In the face of the painful reality (consciously brought to mind by an encounter, scene, word, etc.) of the offensive action, negative shame tries again to register its message of "I am no-good!" with the offender. False in nature, the message of this problematic shame repeatedly tries to strip the offender of their dignity as a human being.

Therefore, the progressive path of emotional healing, through extending forgiveness, can be derailed if negative shame is not processed effectively. That is, it needs to be thwarted and supplanted with a message that, for the offender, affirms that the offense did not represent *the self* that is.

Forgiveness should be recalibrated when there is a struggle to hold on to the release of a debt for both the offended and the offender. Specifically, emotional adjustments must be made in order to retain the forgiveness already extended. There is a need to have another look at the forgiveness extended, with the goal of "pushing" its "reset button." I believe you can appreciate the "reset button"; it is on the microwave appliance and the Internet router box. Critical to "pushing" forgiveness' "reset button," in an effort to recalibrate it, is assessing the gains achieved through extending forgiveness.

Our recalibration processes, however, starts with the understanding that recalibration is a natural phenomenon, post extending forgiveness. We need not lose our composure in facing the task of recalibrating our emotions when it comes to the matter of extended forgiveness. With all the factors that can impact the emotions surrounding the offense carried out against and by us, the struggle to retain the release of a debt should not be viewed as uniquely uncommon.

Like the understanding of keeping negative shame at bay, recalibration of forgiveness must not be viewed as a singular or one-time experience. With a successful recalibration today, there is no absolute guarantee that an individual would not have to recalibrate again tomorrow.

As the struggle to retain the release of a debt can be perpetual, the emotional response of recalibration can be viewed as necessary. In this vein, recalibration can be embraced as a vital part of the enduring work and process of extending forgiveness as one travels the road of emotional healing.

"I know I have forgiven him, but the memory of the offense keeps coming up, reviving those hurtful feelings again, making it difficult for me to hold on to the release that I have so graciously given him." Can you picture this struggle? There is a need for emotional recalibration – a process that includes the indispensable exercise of visiting and acknowledging the gains that accompanied releasing the debtor from their debt.

Since you have forgiven your debtor, you have been less anxious and depressed; able to sleep better throughout the night; able to channel your energy towards positive efforts and endeavors; and, experiencing greater intimacy and value in your interpersonal relationship with the offender.

Overall, you have become less defensive and more of a risk-taker in your relationships. Thoughts of the offense no longer bother you as they once did, which caused you to lose functionality in your day-to-day activities. Generally, you are your *"old self"*; yes, more experienced and alert, but your *"old self."* Your gains even reflect *the self* that is more in harmony with the Creator's ideal for us as human beings.

Emotional Benefits

From the time you have released your debtor, there has been an emotional calm where there might have been anger, a grudge, negative fear, or even a deep-seated hatred towards the offender. Together, these emotions would have provided an emotional cocktail that could have caused a great upheaval in your life, knocking you off course in your progressive path and day-to-day functioning. However, the release of debt emotionally "stabilized" you.

Take note that this release took place because you re-contextualized the offense(s) and the offender. When you released the offender from their debt, the anger subsided, and so did the urge to hold a grudge against them. The thoughts of the offense no longer bother you as functionality has been restored. Consequently, the emotional upheaval caused by the offense(s) was supplanted by an emotional calm and the move back on to the progressive path.

As you "push" the "reset button" in your move towards recalibrating forgiveness, consideration of your current set of emotions, that is keeping you on a progressive path, is of great value. To put it another way, you know where you were emotionally, and you know where you are emotionally; the difference, for you, is like night and day.

This emotional difference may be depicted in a drawing an individual shared in a group session I once facilitated. The session's subject matter brought focus to our ability to choose as human beings and inspired this individual's artistic abilities. The result was a masterful multicolored charcoal drawing showing two optional paths in life that were divided by a road. Sunlight, a bird singing, and a flower in bloom characterized the first option. While darkness, a sad bird, and a wilted flower marked the second option. Emotionally, you were experiencing the dark path, but now you are experiencing the sunlit path.

This brightened path, which is characterized by a set of positive emotions, is also reflected in the laughter of a wife when she received notice of divorce proceedings from her estranged husband. I must admit that I was and still am greatly ignorant of the history of the couple, but I witnessed the receipt of the notification and the wife's subsequent hearty laughter. So, I can only hypothesize about what was emotionally implied in such laughter. This couple had been separated for many years. The spouses moved away from the Creator's ideal for marriage; each ventured into extra-marital affairs, resulting in children outside of their marriage. One could, therefore, only imagine the great emotional flux that both spouses experienced, especially the laughing wife.

However, what the wife's laughter implied was that the emotional upheaval that came with the initial offense(s), which caused the couple to separate, was no longer there. While laughter following the notification of divorce might have been a coping mechanism for the wife, it also suggested that impeding emotions were supplanted by calming progressive ones. I believe this was the case because of the wife's continued functionality after the notification and her responsiveness in signing the divorce papers.

After "pushing" forgiveness' "reset button," you, as the offended, are able to hold on to a set of calming emotions and remain on the path of sunshine, singing birds, and blooming flowers.

Physical Benefits

Physiological gains also must be acknowledged as we consider the recalibration of forgiveness. Our emotional state impacts us physiologically. This is clearly appreciated in the marital sexual encounters shared between a husband and wife. The enjoyment of sexual pleasure that the Creator has provided for a man and a woman, in marriage, comes when they are not distracted, psychologically. Where there is a psychological distraction for them, there is delayed physical/psychological sexual fulfillment. However, the physical gains that come through our psychological state are not limited to the sexual sphere. When we have released the offender from their debt, we will find that our blood pressure, sleep patterns, and energy levels are positively affected.

As indicated earlier, the stress that our physical body goes through, due to hormonal surges caused by anxiety and emotional arousal associated with an offense, is mitigated through the release of the debt. As a result, we feel better and experience improved health. The experience of physical gains, therefore, provides the impetus for the "pushing" of forgiveness' "reset button."

A Progressive Path

The offense brought with it an emotional upheaval in your life. It may have included unforgiveness, due to the injury and loss perpetrated against you. In such an emotional state, energy levels and focus were impacted. Your energy levels along with their focus were diverted from a path characterized by progress, growth, expansion, self-improvement, interest in and the improvement of others, and enhancement of the human experience to a path of stagnation regarding self-growth, growth in others, and general care and concern for your fellow human beings.

However, if there is any benefit the release of the offender's debt brought to your life, it is the redirecting of vital energy levels, bringing focus back to the progressive path. You can tell that you are building again post extending forgiveness. Your life is being added to in your various endeavors.

Additionally, accomplishing your objectives and goals is a reality, as you make valuable contributions to the lives of others. Indeed, progress characterizes your life because your energy resource is now channeled towards the positive.

Such a progressive state feels good as it helps to confirm where you should be, as a human being and as a constituent of the Creator's work. Surely, this progressive state is one that is to be adhered to and vigorously guarded, so that it does not revert to the station in life marked by stagnation. In "pushing" the "reset button" of forgiveness, such a progressive state, realized through the positive focus and channeling of vital energy, will be safeguarded.

Expanded Relational Intimacy and Value

The offense occurred, grace was extended to the offender, forgiveness was meted out, and thus, the relationship with the individual improved. Post forgiveness, there is greater intimacy, along with a deeper understanding and appreciation of the value of the relationship.

Notwithstanding the serious, traumatic, and hurtful nature of certain offenses, if there is any "silver lining" in an offensive situation, it can be experienced on the other side of the offense. It is found in those that leave the relationship intact. Not only intact but better. When the offended and offender work out their differences, deeper levels of intimacy can be achieved – a better understanding of the other's inner psychological processes and feelings can be experienced. This better intimate understanding of the offender by the offended and the offended by the offender augurs well for future engagements in their relationship. Can you agree with this assessment?

The "silver lining" also presents itself in a renewed assessment of the value of the relationship. Sure, the relationship has been tested by the offense; however, both the offended and the offender have passed the test. That is, they have not allowed the offense to dismantle the relationship. Because they persevered, the value of the relationship was brought into focus, through an objective assessment of it. This can be seen in a couple that patiently engages one another following an offending misappropriation of funds. Because of such engagement, moving forward, they now are able to effectively handle monies to achieve their financial goals, while experiencing a renewed appreciation for the value of their relationship.

Such relational enhancements are especially cultivated once the offender demonstrates positive behavioral change in the relationship, and the offended does not pay attention to the offense. Under such dynamics, their relationship is able to progress, reach its full potential, so much so, that it could become an example for others, because of the value or worth that it showcases.

Really, on the post forgiveness side of an offense, one cannot tell the full extent of the positive impact a relationship may have before those observing it. Beyond an offense, others can be advantageously "salted" through a relationship's progressive path that is characterized by a greater intimacy and deeper appreciation of its value by the parties concerned.

It is the gains, seen in greater relational intimacy and value that motivate "pushing" the "reset button" of forgiveness - when there is a struggle to retain release of the offender's debt. Recall the newfound levels of intimacy the relationship experiences and its "polished" worth that got its chance to be showcased through the offense! You will find that the recalibration of forgiveness has a greater chance of being a part of your experience and reality.

Freedom in Risk and Vulnerability

Since you have forgiven your debtor, you have become less defensive and have once again started to take risks in your relationships. Through your risk-taking, you have become more vulnerable, for you are now appropriately revealing more of your inner self to those who are a part of your interpersonal relationships.

Because you know the value and benefits attached to taking risks and being appropriately vulnerable, you also know that this is or can be a good place for you to be. You realize that the relational gains are predicated on risk-taking and vulnerability. The positive, progressive path that you are on is undergirded by your risk-taking as well as by your vulnerability. Because you have become less defensive, you are now able to venture out as a vulnerable risk-taker in your relationships. Also, you have attained a measure of freedom. You are "unfettered" or "unchained," as you move towards the full potential of your relational experiences. In your defensive mood, and in the absence of taking risks and being vulnerable, such freedom was not yours.

However, since you released the offender from their debt, you are now benefitting from the bestowals of being a risk-taker who is not reticent, and responsibly so, in revealing more of yourself to others, as they do to you. Consequently, you know that this quality in your life is something that should be preserved. Recalibrating forgiveness by "pushing" its "reset button," will help ensure that you continue in the freedom and benefits of being a vulnerable risk-taker.

Functioning in the Creator's Ideal

In forgiving the offender, you have demonstrated one of the qualities of the Creator. You may recall that He is quite involved with the process of forgiveness, for He has provided a sacrifice, in His Son, that allows Him to release us from our debts through offenses against Him. He provides an ideal model, in Himself, for us when it comes to the task of forgiving offenders. In this model, the Creator also provides the inspiration and encouragement for us as we release our debtors from their debts.

Like your Creator, you have forgiven the offense of your offender. While there may be other areas in your life that are wanting, when compared to the Creator's overall nature, or what He has called you to, still, to forgive, as He forgives is commendable. Moreover, having forgiven your offender, you share in His ideal for humanity. The Creator desires and expects us to forgive our fellow human beings when they offend us. Because we know how beneficial extending forgiveness can be to our interpersonal relationships, we can appreciate why there exists such an expectation.

To be like the Creator, functioning in this ideal of forgiving an offender is a posture that should be retained, especially if it can be perceived as a starting point in a complete journey towards the Creator.

What is implied here concerning losing the struggle to retain the release of the offender's debt, particularly, when the emotion of unforgiveness is allowed to resurface, is the danger of embracing a position that is not in harmony with the Creator's nature. In "pushing" forgiveness' "reset button," the offended has an opportunity to adhere to a noble quality that belongs to the Creator.

The Offender's Emotional Healing

As you reflect on the offensive situation, you can identify that since its occurrence and your release of the offender from their debt, you have experienced a degree of emotional healing. Your life is being rebuilt on its progressive path. Your relationship, even with the offender, is healthier. You have expanded, experientially. Indeed, because you navigated the offense and are experiencing the benefits that the process brought to your life, you are better off. I want to remind you that the person you forgave, the one who offended you, might also be better off, as they experience your grace.

As offenders exhibit genuine behavioral change, post the offense(s), and demonstrate that they value the relationship, they will expand and mature in their personhood and interconnected relationships – so they too are on a progressive path. Surely, to see individuals who have failed in their interpersonal relationships and in their relationship with their Creator, get back up, follow the protocol regarding forgiveness, and get on the path of healing, is a glorious thing to behold.

When recalibration of forgiveness occurs, it is in harmony with a spirit that extends goodwill to others, promotes the wellbeing of others, and that desires their emotional healing.

"Pushing" forgiveness' "reset button" further establishes personal and relational gains your offender experienced in having been forgiven. It also encourages them to take the path where they could avoid those behaviors that interfere with their harmonious interpersonal relationships.

The gains, through extending forgiveness, run the entire gamut of what constitutes our self-worth or sense of wellbeing. Such gains directly impact our psychological, physical, social, and spiritual health.

Proposed in this chapter is the need to recalibrate forgiveness to ensure that you continue to prosper in all aspects of your life as an individual who has been the object or perpetrator of an offense(s).

For further deliberation…

1. Extending forgiveness is a process that goes beyond the release of the offender's debt. Do you agree? Why or why not?

2. Should we be comfortable with having to adjust or recalibrate after forgiving an offender emotionally?

3. The gains acquired after extending forgiveness are considerations in recalibrating forgiveness. How important are they?

4. Greater intimacy in a relationship and a "polished" value of it are significant gains to consider when recalibrating forgiveness. Do you think these are the greatest gains? Why or why not?

5. Is there any tension between the gains of the offended and those of the offender when recalibration of forgiveness takes place?

I Forgive

Chapter Eleven

Minimizing Offense

It is almost that time when I will advise you to unbuckle your seatbelt because our journey to the frontier of forgiveness has come to an end. However, I believe that it is crucial before we end our time together, that I provide some principles that can help us reduce some of the offenses that we perpetrate against each other. Indeed, some offenses need not happen if certain principles are operational in our lives!

As we have seen, one of the main reasons why we offend is we are intolerant of one another's viewpoints and behaviors, particularly when there is an insistence that "My view is right," and "Your actions are wrong." However, there are a lot of situations and circumstances where certain perspectives and behaviors are not a matter of right or wrong. We can identify such situations and circumstances as being on "neutral ground" where all parties can be "right" in their perspectives and behaviors.

I recall visiting a Dollar Tree store in the United States. At that time, there was one cashier on duty, so the checkout line had become very long. There was another employee of the company, a manager, taking a break outside the store, in clear view of the cashier. He came in from his break, noticed the long line of customers waiting to be served, and said to the cashier, "You could have called me to help you." However, the cashier retorted, "You could have seen that I needed help."

In my estimation, both were "right" in their perspectives. Surely, the manager, seeing the long line, could have shortened his break, and the cashier could have paused briefly and called the manager. But what if the manager had persisted that he should have been called, after the customers in the long line had been served? And what if the cashier also persisted in the view that the manager should have seen that help was needed at the checkout line? We can see where this could lead – to one or both being accused of being wrong, and/or one or both becoming offended.

Such offenses can be avoided though if there is an acknowledgment that all parties can be "right" in their views on the matter and a decision be made to let the situation "die." By the way, I believe this was the outcome of the situation with Dollar Tree's employees, for it seemed to have "died" after their short exchange. If this was the case, they acted commendably in not pushing their individual perspectives, while, at the same time, indirectly acknowledging that there was no right or wrong in the situation, for both parties were "right."

Perhaps, a set of signs can help us further appreciate that there are other perspectives or worldviews that exist, which may be different from ours. The signs are not necessarily opposing or wrong. Rather, they underscore that there are different perspectives that can co-exist among us.

While I was exiting the parking lot of an establishment, the exit led to a one-way street. Posted on the pillars of the exit gate were two signs. One read "No left turn" and the other read, "Right turn only" (*see figure 14*). A careful study of these signs revealed that they conveyed the same message – both directed drivers into the route of the one-way street.

We see then *the principle of respect* for the other person's "right" view, as an important consideration in minimizing offenses. It is a principle that has inherent within it the understanding that my view is not the only view on many matters. Because my view may be different from that of another, it does not mean that it is necessarily right and that theirs is necessarily wrong for all views can be "right."

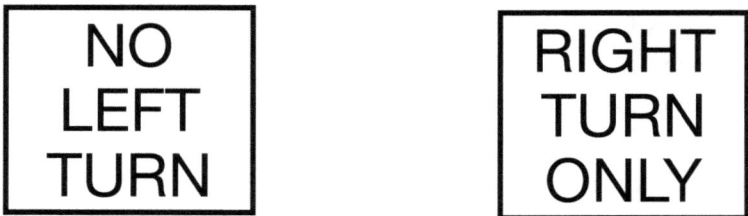

NO
LEFT
TURN

RIGHT
TURN
ONLY

Figure 14 – *The Co-existence of Difference*

Consequently, there is no need to argue such views until they convince me, or I convince them. It must be emphasized here that I am talking primarily about opinionated matters, views that have their footing outside the Creator's expressed code for our lives. In that which constitutes a major part of what I have been referring to as our mutual moral "oughtness."

An appropriate question that can help us respect the other person's view is, "Can her view co-exist with mine?" Or, "Can it stand side by side with my worldview?" We must remember that it is through our different worldviews or the "guiding lenses" through which we see things, that we find our unique contributions that build relationships and society, overall.

Our worldviews have been individually and uniquely crafted during our developing years. In most instances, worldviews enable individuals to present to society as functional and productive. Because of the adaptations within our developmental environments, and the worldviews they have produced, we see things differently and, therefore, we behave differently. Again, such differences do not necessarily have to be right or wrong.

Sometimes, when shopping together, I have to tell my wife that she has a "case mentality." An explanation for this is that she grew up on a family island that is separate from the "big city," where she now resides. Therefore, her family had to purchase their groceries in bulk or cases from the stores in the city when they visited. Even though she now lives in the city, when shopping, she still talks about buying a case of something.

During our shopping experience, the way she thinks is different from the way I think. In my thinking, I want to let the dollar cover as much "grounds" as possible – an event that would be impeded by spending it on a case of something. You can call my mindset when grocery shopping the "stretch mentality." I want to get as much variety in with the grocery items, as the dollar will allow. So, there is the "case mentality" and the "stretch mentality." When they meet, they can become a possible "breeding ground" for conflict and offense, if they are not respected as two different ways of thinking stemming from two different worldviews, that are not necessarily right or wrong.

I want to go a bit further with this idea of having respect for the varying perspectives of those who comprise our interpersonal relationships. You may know that the driving experience can be another "breeding ground" for tension, conflict, and offenses between occupants in the vehicle, especially husbands and wives. The speed, how, and when other drivers are engaged, the route to a destination, when to fill-up with gas, and parking options can all lead to an offense when respect for the driver's "right" view is absent. I am not talking about appropriate suggestions, advice, or counsel offered during the driving experience. I am talking about one occupant insisting that the driver's driving makes "no sense" when it can be respected.

If we ask, "Can his view on the route co-exist with mine?" It probably would make "plenty (tolerable) sense." Take note that there is no essential difference between Route A and Route B in *figure 15*. The goal is to get to the food store, and both routes will get shoppers there at almost the same time.

Offenses can also be diminished if, instead of approaching a situation with a presupposed judgment, we approach it by asking questions. Sometimes, as "clear" as a situation may seem at first, by asking questions about it, initial views, based on the answers given, may be inaccurate. Offenses can be avoided if we ask questions: Is this what I am seeing? Can you explain your actions? What do you mean? How could I have responded differently, in your view? Maybe, I am missing something, but why did you say that? Is there more to his actions? Is there more to her words?

We can call this principle, *the principle of inquiry*. Through it, we come to appreciate a broader picture of what may be going on beyond the surface of the situation. It affords us the opportunity to judge rightly, and therefore, respond appropriately. It also provides an easier path when giving the other party the benefit of the doubt; you know that the other party values the relationship, so, there must be something else going on, beyond what you see or hear that may appear to be problematic for the relationship.

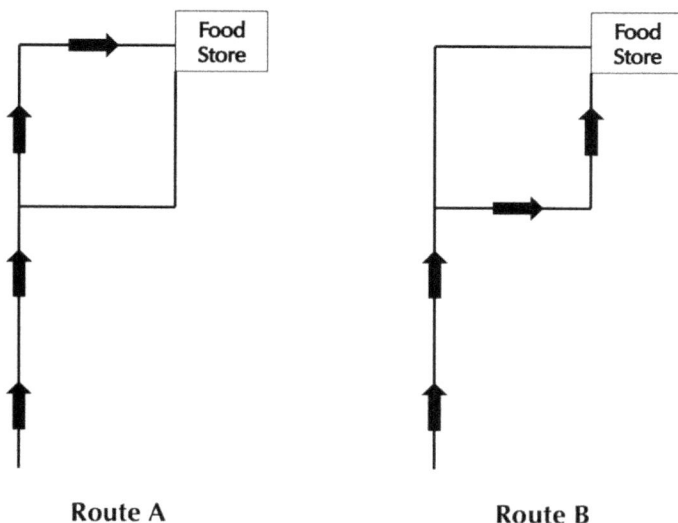

Route A   **Route B**

Figure 15 – *A Trip to the Food Store*

The principle also keeps parties better informed whenever a questionable situation arises within the relationship, which further keeps them out of the circle of offenses.

Indispensable to minimizing offenses is patience. Parties in a relationship should endure or bear with one another. I know it is challenging at times to retain, but this quality is needed to maintain the value and longevity of our interpersonal relationships.

Please do not be grossed out over the illustration that I am about to use! I believe there is useful utility in it as focus is brought to bear on this term called patience. I want to direct your attention to the phenomenon of passing gas or flatulence, a ubiquitous human experience. All human beings experience it! The experience is, for the most part, private, controlled, and regulated in our interpersonal experiences. If this is not the case, then it can also become very offensive. This was the case with an individual who deliberately passed gas in the cabin of an airplane, as it traveled through the airspaces to its destination. I believe you can see how this would be offensive to the other passengers.

There was an occasion, while traveling with some male classmates, from Tennessee to Arkansas, that one of them silently "cut loose." I indicated to my traveling companions that we had gone to another level of intimacy when I realized what had occurred. One of them, in a tone that revealed he was displeased and offended by the experience, indicated he was not ready for such intimacy. His response prompted an apology from the originator of the "bad gas." However, with those in our close relational circles, passing gas is seen and accepted as the norm. It can even be viewed as a path to a deepened intimacy, as indicated earlier.

On another occasion, while journeying in a vehicle (the windows were up), with two of my female cohort members, one of them silently "cut loose." After a period of exposure and silence, I remarked, "So, we have moved to another level of intimacy." There was no response to the remark. I believe they agreed with the sentiment. Or maybe there was just great reluctance on behalf of the originator to own up to the responsibility of the event.

Sometimes, because of the unpleasant nature of the "bad gas," it can significantly disrupt or disturb our valued relationships to such an extent that the parties may begin to ask salient questions like, "What's going on?" and "Do you need to use the bathroom?" There may also be a strong suggestion made: "You need a cleaning out!"

Yet, no matter how odoriferous the gas, the party it came from is endured. Why? Because today it is the other person, but tomorrow it will be you, for passing odorous gas is no respecter of persons. Since you know what it is like to be patient in the uncomfortable and unpleasant situations involving passing gas, universalize the quality, as you encounter the other unpleasant moments in your interpersonal relationships! Thank you for enduring the passing gas illustrations!

We can call this indispensable principle, *the principle of endurance*. Patience, like asking questions and having respect for the other party's "rights," is a proactive quality that helps to ward off acting or speaking in an offensive way. Like the principle of inquiry, the principle of endurance works to illuminate the situation for parties in a relationship. The more one is patient with their friend, boss, wife, husband, parent, child, and fellow employee, the more one can see and stay out of the offending path or circle of offense.

Minimizing offense will not be complete without bringing the boundaries that are found in our interpersonal relationships into focus. Often, when offense occurs, it is through a disregard for others; that is, their person, property, sacred space, relationships, and personal business. This can be seen when there is an encroachment or intrusion on the possessions or privacy of others. In offense, boundaries are breached and the "outcry" of their limiting "No!" is not heeded or respected.

In a case where hospitality went wrong, this was highlighted. We will call our host Ann. She has a number of rental units and spare rooms at her home. She also has a kind heart that allows her to give lodging to those in need until their circumstances change for the better. On one such occasion, Ann exclaimed, "Please put me out of my misery. Someone, please knock me in the head next time I offer someone, ANYONE, a place to live." This statement came from Ann because someone, one of her guests, stole everything from one of her living quarters and lied about it.

The individual who stole Ann's belongings showed a disregard for her and breached the boundary surrounding her property, plundering her possessions. Consequently, an offense was perpetrated against Ann to such an extent that she resolved not to offer "ANYONE, a place to live." I sympathize with Ann. What happened to her should not have happened! The thief should have heeded the "outcry" of the boundaries, with their limiting "No!" that surrounded Ann's possessions.

This brings us to *the principle of respect for the boundaries of others.* It is a principle that is so important to know and apply if we want to stay out of the circle of offense. The principle takes into consideration the boundaries of others. It acknowledges that they do exist, and for a good reason – they help protect the possessions of others. Therefore, boundaries can be seen as keepers of our mutual moral "oughtness" – they help us to respond to each other appropriately.

Some possessions deserve so much protection that, if we look carefully, we can "see" more than one boundary around them. This is revealed in a stringent protocol that permits toddlers to be picked up from kindergartens by individuals other than their parents. For such individuals, they need to show IDs and, perhaps, provide a signed authorization note from the parents. Additionally, there may be a need to make a phone call to the parents authorizing the caregivers to release the precious toddlers to those collecting them.

A ring on her finger, the wearing of his name, and a reference to her husband, provide clear boundaries around a beautiful woman. They exclaim to the one smitten by her attractiveness that, "She is off limits!" and "She belongs to another!" Therefore, to advance oneself towards her, in an improper way, would lead to offense.

This principle informs us that others have to invite us in, as they open up to us and uncover sacred dimensions of *the self* that are ordinarily off limits. Such a principle encourages us to obtain permission. It directs us to get the nod first, before we lay hold of another's property or before we engage them over personal matters.

Getting permission before we enter someone's personal space has some advantages. It helps individuals to understand the value and nature of the relationship, as well as provide the assurance that issues can be dealt with openly without having to wonder if one intruded into an area in the relationship where one does not belong.

More than anything, the principle of respect for the boundaries of others reminds us that not everything in our interpersonal relationships is accessible to us. To help us avoid the circle of offense, there is a need for us to be content and not lose our composure when we encounter the boundaries of others and the limiting "No!" they exclaim.

With minimizing offense in mind, it is incumbent upon us to reflect on the Creator. Remember, we can offend Him! So, how do we minimize offenses against our Creator? Possessing knowledge of His code of conduct for humanity is indispensable if we wish to pursue this goal successfully. His code of conduct, which is found in the Bible, will help us avoid offensive behaviors perpetrated directly against Him and through our interpersonal relationships with our fellow human beings.

At this juncture, though, it is important to understand that knowing what is offensive to the Creator is one thing, but being forgiven by Him is another. We have already seen in a previous chapter, how and when the Creator forgives.

I can know what is required to please the Creator, through searching and accurate handling of the words found in the Bible. This knowledge must be combined with compliant faith: "And without faith it is impossible to please Him, for he who comes to God must believe that He is and that He is a rewarder of those who seek Him" (Hebrews 11:6); "For just as the body without the spirit is dead, so also faith without works is dead" (James 2:26).

Compliant faith takes individuals beyond mental assent to incorporating, practically, the code of the Creator in their lives. To know is one thing, but to act is another! To be persuaded is one thing, but to allow that persuasion to shape our lives, is another. Pleasing the Creator is inextricably linked to knowing and doing His will. And just as both qualities are linked to pleasing Him, they are also linked to minimizing offenses against Him.

In this last chapter, I have sought to present some principles that could help us to minimize offenses against our Creator and those in our interpersonal relationships. It was not an exhaustive presentation, and perhaps, you can think about other principles that are important to reducing the number of offenses that cross our paths. Remember, if governing principles are already at work in our lives, they can help us avoid the words or actions that would cause problematic hindrances and hurdles in our relationships.

You might have noticed that the principles shared apply to "you," the individual. When I/we respect the "rights" of others, ask questions in troubling situations, exercise patience with others, and respect their boundaries, I am, or we are less prone to offend them.

For further deliberation…

1. You might have or heard of an unscrupulous employer or spouse. What impact would the behavior of such an individual have on your interpersonal relationships?

2. Can you reflect on the co-existence of different worldviews and its importance to minimizing offenses?

3. How many ways can a meal of macaroni and cheese be prepared?

4.   Why would seeking clarity to the words or actions of a partner be important to a relationship?

5.   In our interpersonal relationships, not everything is accessible to us. What might this fact be telling you?

6.   Should we be concerned about offending the Creator? Why or why not?

Conclusion

A major factor that has huge implications for us as participants in the human experience, and as we consider our world of offenses, is our sense of duty regarding behavior towards each other. Such a duty has been defined as our mutual moral "oughtness." Universally seen in societies, it receives greater definition through an understanding of the Creator's biblical code for our lives. If it did not exist, then certain offenses in our interpersonal relationships and relationship with our Creator would not exist. It is a breach in this mutual moral "oughtness" that leads us to offend the Creator and one another.

At the backdrop of offenses is our desire and need for human connectedness. Because we strive for it and greater intimacy in our relational spheres, we expose ourselves to the possibility of being offended. Whether such offenses are intentional, inadvertent, or otherwise, they can hinder the harmony striven for in our interpersonal relationships and the relationship with our Creator. However, while some offenses are universal in nature, some are unique to a relationship, and then there are others, as they would impact human relations, that do not reach the level where they disrupt a harmonious relationship with the Creator.

The consequences of certain offenses can be long lasting, especially those that are marked by severe trauma. The emotional pain and hurt can also create functional hindrances and sometimes those experiencing these challenges need psychological professionals to help them.

Loss also accompanies offense and such losses stir the emotional resources that have been given to us by the Creator to help us adapt in life. Anger is one of these resources, which can be very advantageous to us. Particularly, when there is injustice, and when it is managed properly. Yet, anger can digress to a state of emotional unforgiveness, when there is a grudge held against those who offend us. Unforgiveness takes its toll on us though, acting as a kind of burdensome yoke. It negatively impacts our functionality – emotionally, socially, mentally, physically, and spiritually. It is important to underscore that unforgiveness also interferes with a harmonious relationship with our Creator.

Notwithstanding the upheaval or emotional pain that an offense can bring to our lives, we have seen that such pain can be reduced, and an individual can be healed from the wound of an offense by extending forgiveness to his or her offender. Extending forgiveness is a choice that helps to restore our functionality in many dimensions of our human experience. It also involves managing our emotional state where we steer away from negative ones and embrace positives emotions.

While we know that there are great gains to forgiving an offender, sometimes it is difficult to do so. Help is needed! Such help comes through being empathetic towards those who have offended us. We reach a state of empathy, as we would gain a different perspective of the offense and the offender. With such an empathetic perspective, we can decide to release offenders from their debt(s) towards us that came with the offense(s) they perpetrated against us.

Extending forgiveness should not occur in a vacuum. Other considerations that accompany this process, such as the safety of the individual who has been offended, should not be withstood. There is a responsible dimension that is attached to extending forgiveness and it should not be discounted. Also, the invaluable advantages that are attached to the process should not be ignored, especially because of the primary benefits available to the offended and the gains that the offender may experience.

Moreover, our study of certain biblical characters provided us with a group of individuals, who have processed their offense(s) admirably. If there is any consolation in the struggle to forgive an offender, it is seen in the fact that the challenge is not unique to a single individual; it is a pervasive phenomenon. But the biblical characters have also set a precedent for us, in that, notwithstanding the intensity of the emotional hurt brought on by offenses, they can be forgiven; it is possible not to pay attention to an offense.

More than the biblical characters, in our own contemporary context, we can find individuals who have become exemplars for us in our process of extending forgiveness. They serve to motivate, fuel the courage, and imbue the cognitive reality and feeling of competency in, "If they can do it, then so can I" when it comes to forgiving an offender.

There is no greater modeling regarding how we should extend forgiveness than that which is demonstrated by our Creator. Sure, we see the conditional requirements that are attached to the forgiveness that He offers offenders, but this is connected to His comprehensive functions, including that of Judge for humanity. Yet, because He participates in the experience of extending forgiveness, the Creator, through the display of His character qualities, also encourages us to follow the path of releasing our offenders from their debts, incurred through their offenses.

Our process of extending forgiveness brings into focus the value and worth of offenders. Appreciating their value, can position us to become empathetic towards them, and subsequently, release them from their debts. We must remember that human value, marred by the perpetration of an offense, is not tantamount to negation of such a value.

There are many conditions that work to help us release our debtors from the debts that they incurred when they perpetrated offenses against us. If we are open, alert, and flexible we will find that some offenders say, through their words and actions, that they are sorry for the wrong they have committed against us and they still desire to be in a relationship. Given such conditions, some offenders make it easier for the offended to not pay attention to the offenses perpetrated against them.

The process of extending forgiveness is not limited to the offended releasing offenders from their debts. Offenders can share in it also, particularly, when they forgive themselves for the offense(s) that they have perpetrated against others. Actually, for emotional healing to occur in their lives, offenders need to be able to forgive themselves. They need to be aware of the reality that their offensive behaviors do not define or encapsulate them as individuals. Indeed, their worth as human beings supersedes their offenses! Fulfillment of purpose and potential can still be within their reach, even though they have committed offense(s).

Therefore, it is important for offenders to understand that they too can become objects of emotional healing. Not necessarily or merely coming from others, who demonstrate concern for them, but such healing emotions, like compassion, should come from *the self* towards *the self*.

The compassion that targets *the self*, helps offenders to release themselves from protracted psychological and damaging guilt that comes in its various forms, as well as other encaging emotions, including unforgiveness.

Additionally, both the offended and offender can extend forgiveness. After all, there is a need for emotional healing for the individual who was offended and for the one who perpetrated the offense.

With all that is wrong with our world today, it is good to know that extending forgiveness provides a refreshing option, amidst the negativity. It has the potential to shape successive generations as it is seen and embraced as a lifestyle. Its value must, therefore, not be discounted; rather, those releasing their offenders from their debts should appreciate that they are setting a noble precedent for the next generation.

The process of extending forgiveness must also be viewed as foundational for a relationship that has been damaged by an offense, particularly as it moves towards renewal. Relational pillars such as respect and trust find their repair and revival through extending forgiveness.

Following an offense, it is very difficult to retain the value of a relationship without extending forgiveness. This process then is critical to placing the relationship on a path of healing and relational harmony.

This work acknowledges the struggle that individuals experience as they seek to forgive those who have offended them. I believe that it has offered a helpful advantage in the process. However, such a struggle may not end with the courageous move of forgiving one's offender. Yet, there is recourse through making the necessary emotional adjustments, in the process of recalibration, so that we can keep those forgiven in a state of "release of debt." These emotional adjustments take place as both the offended and the offender revisit the benefits afforded through extending forgiveness.

While there is help in reaching the point where we extend, receive, and retain forgiveness, there are certain principles that help us to minimize the offense(s) in our interpersonal relationships. As we consider relational harmony, if we do not have to offend in the first place, then we should avoid it! We can avoid it!

Often, offenses come from our inaccurate view of the situations. Consequently, we sometimes respond in ways that are offensive. So, principles such as endurance and inquiry can go a long way in assisting us to avoid the circle of offense.

It is hoped that this work has provided key considerations and resources that can help you release your offender(s) from the debt(s) incurred through the offense(s) perpetrated against you. This can be very challenging, but it is doable! I believe that the resources offered in this work, although they are not exhaustive, once applied, can aid you tremendously!

I guess you can tell that we are reaching the end of our time together. But maybe not, as you determine within yourself to reread this work and further glean principles that you might have missed during your first read! Either way, it is appropriate for me to tell you that you can now "unbuckle your seatbelt" for our journey together, to the frontier of forgiveness, has come to an end.

However, we cannot part ways before I reveal a bit further about what happened to Karen Woodside. My alliance with Karen, in a clinical setting, came to an end. She had reached a point where she no longer blamed herself for the injustice perpetrated by her husband against their daughter.

She moved on with her life and took a liberating road trip where she reconnected with family and old acquaintances. She also got on with living, as she searched to secure a new place of abode for her family. Karen's moving on with life, along with completing the therapy sessions, was a clear indication that she had found the help she needed to navigate the struggle she had to forgive her husband. It was also apparent that the yoke of unforgiveness no longer impeded her functionality!

I leave you with two stories that we can place before us, as examples and motivation in our efforts to forgive those who offend us! First, in revealing inspiring stories of extreme forgiveness, *Reader's Digest* highlighted an interview that they designated or called, *The Unexpected*

Caregiver.[9] It was published in *Real Simple.* The interview was with Pascale Kavanagh, who had experienced violent abuse at the hands of her mother, during her formative years. Hatred had developed towards her mother and there was a relational disconnection between the two.

However, as time went on, Kavanagh's mother suffered a series of strokes that took away her capacity to communicate and care for herself. Because there was no one besides Kavanagh to care for her mother, she assumed the responsibility. Through reading to her mother on a regular basis, while she sat by her bedside, Kavanagh revealed that the hatred that she had had towards her mother vanished – it was supplanted by forgiveness and love.

Our second story involves Brandt Jean. During a victim's impact statement, Jean extended forgiveness to Amber Guyger who was convicted of murdering his older brother, Botham Jean. In an unexpected and unscripted turn of events, Brandt spoke from his heart about forgiveness.

In speaking, although Brandt might have misrepresented regarding how and when the Creator forgives (**see chapter on *When The Creator Forgives***), yet he provides for us a good example of what it means to extend forgiveness, as he released Amber Guyger from the debt she incurred in murdering his brother.

In Brandt's case, he verbalized his forgiveness towards Amber on the stand. He said, "I forgive you!" Additionally, he expressed that he wanted the best for her and did not want her to go to jail. He even asked the judge (actually pleaded with her) for an opportunity to give Amber a hug. When the request was granted, he descended the witness stand and walked towards Amber. She, in turn, ran to Brandt from where she sat. In a beautiful and gracious moment, both of them embraced for an extended time in the middle of the courtroom, as they exchanged inaudible words, which were, most likely, in harmony with the forgiveness extended.

While Amber left the courtroom to start her prison term, it is quite understandable that enduring such a term is made easier as she benefits psychologically and emotionally from the forgiveness she received from Brandt Jean.

May you be blessed in your pursuit of the Creator, and may He help you in your desire and need to forgive those who have offended you!

Endnotes

Chapter 1

1. Susan Johnson, "Extravagant Emotion: Understanding and Transforming Love Relationships in Emotionally Focused Therapy," in *The Healing Power of Emotion: Affective Neuroscience, Development & Clinical Practice*, eds. Diana Fosha, Daniel J. Siegel, and Marion F. Solomon (W.W. Norton & Company: New York, 2009), 262-266.

2. Francine Shapiro and Louise Maxfield, "EMDR and Information Processing in Psychotherapy Treatment: Personal Development and Global Implications," in Healing Trauma: Attachment, Mind, Body, and Brain, eds. Marion F. Solomon and Daniel J. Siegel (W.W. Norton & Company: New York, 2003), 198-199.

3. Ibid.

4. Diana Fosha, "Dyadic Regulation and Experiential Work with Emotion and Relatedness in Trauma and Disorganized Attachment," in Healing Trauma: Attachment, Mind, Body, and Brain, eds. Marion F. Solomon and Daniel J. Siegel (W.W. Norton & Company: New York, 2003), 230-276.

5. Francine Shapiro and Louise Maxfield, "EMDR and Information Processing in Psychotherapy Treatment: Personal Development and Global Implications," in Healing Trauma: Attachment, Mind, Body, and Brain, eds. Marion F. Solomon and Daniel J. Siegel (W.W. Norton & Company: New York, 2003), 196-217.

Chapter 2

6. Charlotte vanOyen Witvliet, Thomas E. Ludwig, and Kelly L. Vander Laan, "Granting Forgiveness Or Harboring Grudges: Implications for Emotion, Physiology, and Health," Psychological Science 12, no.2 (2001): 122, https://journals.sagepub.com.

Chapter 3

7. Laura Schlessinger, 10 Stupid Things Women Do To Mess Up Their Lives (New York: Quill, 2002), 197.

Chapter 8

8. Blake M. Riek, "Transgressions, guilt, and forgiveness: a model of seeking forgiveness," Journal Of Psychology & Theology 38, no. 4 (2010): 253, ATLASerials, Religion Collection, EBSCOhost.

Conclusion

9. Stephanie Booth, "3 True Stories of Forgiveness," Real Simple, (2014): https://www.realsimple.com/work-life/life-strategies/inspiration-motivation/stories-forgiveness?

Bibliography

Bassett, Rodney L., Kelly M. Bassett, Matthew W. Lloyd, and Jason L. Johnson. "Seeking Forgiveness: Considering the Role of Moral Emotions." *Journal of Psychology and Theology* 34, no. 2 (June 1, 2006): 111.https://search.ebscohost.com/login.aspx?direct=true&-AuthType=ip&db=edo&AN=ejs44828956&scope=site.

Baur, L, J Duffy, E Fountain, S Halling, M Holzer, E Jones, M Leifer, and J O Rowe. "Exploring Self Forgiveness." *Journal Of Religion And Health* 31, no. 2 (June 1992): 149-160. doi:10.1007/BF00986793.

Booth, Stephanie. "3 True Stories of Forgiveness." *Real Simple*, (2014): https://www.realsimple.com/work-life/life-strategies/inspiration-motivation/stories=forgiveness?

Cerling, Charles E. "Some Thoughts on A Biblical View of Anger: A Response." *Journal of Psychology and Theology* 2, no. 4 (September 1, 1974): 266.https://search.ebscohost.com/login.aspx?direct=true&-AuthType=ip&db=edo&AN=ejs44832593&scope=site.

Cowley, Christopher. "Why Genuine Forgiveness must be Elective and Unconditional." *Ethical Perspectives* 17, no. 4 (December 2010): 556-79. doi:10.2143/EP.17.4.2059846.

Davis, James R., and Gregg J. Gold. "An examination of emotional empathy, attributions of stability, and the link between perceived remorse and forgiveness." *Personality and Individual Differences* 50, no. 3 (2011): 392-97. doi:10.1016/j.paid.2010.10.031.

Dionisio, Guillermo R. "Paul Ricoeur's Antropolgy of Forgiveness." *Budhi: A Journal of Ideas and Culture* 20, no. 2 (2016): 118-44. *ATLASerials, Religion Collection*, EBSCO*host*.

Duff, Nancy J., and Gordon S. Mikoski. "On the Complexities of Forgiveness." *Theology Today* 69. no. 4 (January 2013): 381. doi:10.1177/0040573612463128.

Fehr, Ryan, Michele J. Gelfand, and Monisha Nag. "The Road to Forgiveness: A Meta-Analytic Synthesis of Its Situational and Dispositional Correlates." *Psychological Bulletin* 136, no. 5 (September 1, 2010): 894–914. https://search.ebscohost.com/login.aspx?direct=true&AuthType=ip&db=eric&AN=EJ896350&scope=site.

Fincham, Frank D., F. Giorgia Paleari, and Camillo Regalia. "Forgiveness in marriage: The role of relationship quality, attributions, and empathy." *Personal Relationships* 9, no. 1 (March 2002): 27-37. doi:10.1111/1475-6811.00002.

Finkel, Eli J., Caryl E. Rusbult, Madoka Kumashiro, and Peggy A. Hannon. "Dealing With Betrayal in Close Relationships: Does Commitment Promote Forgiveness?" *Journal of Personality & Social Psychology* 82, no. 6 (June 2002): 956–74. doi:10.1037/0022-3514.82.6.956.

Fredrickson, Barbara L., Michele M. Tugade, Christian E. Waugh, and Gregory R. Larkin, "What Good Are Positive Emotions in Crisis? A Prospective Study of Resilience and Emotions Following the Terrorist Attacks on the United States on September 11th, 2001." *Journal of Personality & Social Psychology* 84, no. 2 (February 2003): 365–76. doi:10.1037/0022-3514.84.2.365.

Frise, Nathan R., and Mark R. Mcminn. "Forgiveness and Reconciliation: The Differing Perspectives of Psychologists and Christian Theologians." *Journal of Psychology and Theology* 38, no. 2 (June 1, 2010): 83. https://search.ebscohost.com/login.aspx?direct=true&AuthType=ip&db=edo&AN=ejs44827806&scope=site.

Fosha, Diana. "Dyadic Regulation and Experiential Work with Emotion and Relatedness in Trauma and Disorganized Attachment." In *Healing Trauma: Attachment, Mind, Body, and Brain*, edited by Marion F. Solomon and Daniel J. Siegel, 230-76. New York: W.W. Norton & Company, 2003.

Green, Melanie C., Geoff Kaufman, Mary Flanagan, and Kaitlin Fitzgerald. "Self-esteem and public self-consciousness moderate the emotional impact of expressive writing about experiences with bias." *Personality and Individual Differences* 116, (October 2017): 212-15. doi:10.1016/j.paid.2017.04.057.

Hall, Julie H., and Frank D. Fincham. "Relationship Dissolution Following Infidelity: The Roles of Attributions and Forgiveness." *Journal of Social & Clinical Psychology* 25, no. 5 (May 2006): 508–22. doi:10.1521/jscp.2006.25.5.508.

————. "The Temporal Course of Self-Forgiveness." *Journal of Social & Clinical Psychology* 27, no. 2 (February 2008): 174–202. doi:10.1521/jscp.2008.27.2.174.

Harris, Alex H.S., and Carl E. Thoresen. "Forgiveness, Unforgiveness, Health and Disease." In *Handbook of Forgiveness*, edited by Everett L. Worthington Jr., 321-33. New York: Routledge, 2005.

Jennings, David J., Everett L. Worthington, Daryl R. Van Tongeren, Johua N. Hook, Don E. Davis, Audrey L.

Gartner, Chelsea L. Greer, and David K. Mosher. "The Transgressor's Response to Denied Forgiveness." *Journal of Psychology and Theology* 44, no. 1 (March 1, 2016): 16. https://search.ebscohost.com/login.aspx?direct=true&AuthType=ip&db=edo&AN=e-js44827954&scope=site.

Johnson, Susan. "Extravagant Emotion: Understanding and Transforming Love Relationships in Emotionally Focused Therapy." In *The Healing Power of Emotion: Affective Neuroscience, Development & Clinical Practice*, edited by Diana Fosha, Daniel J. Siegel, and Marion F. Solomon, 262-66. New York: W.W. Norton & Company, 2009.

Karremans, Johan C., and Paul A.M. Van Lange. "Does activating justice help or hurt in promoting forgiveness?" *Journal of Experimental Social Psychology* 41, no. 3 (2005): 290-97. doi:10.1016/j.jesp.2004.06.005.

_____., Paul A. M. Van Lange, Jaap W. Ouwerkerk, and Esther S. Kluwar. "When Forgiving Enhances Psychological Well-Being: The Role of Interpersonal Commitment." *Journal of Personality & Social Psychology* 84, no. 5 (May 2003): 1011–26. doi:10.1037/0022-3514.84.5.1011.

Kim, Jichan J., and Robert D. Enright. "A Theological and Psychological Defense of Self-Forgiveness: Implications for Counseling." *Journal of Psychology and Theology* 42. no. 3 (September 1, 2014); 260. https://search.ebscohost.com/login.aspx?direct=true&AuthType=ip&db=edo&AN=ejs44828719&scope=site.

Lauritzen, Paul. "Forgiveness: moral prerogative or religious duty?" *Journal of Religious Ethics* 15, no. 2 (1987): 141-54. *ATLASerials, Religion Collection*, EBSCO*host*.

Luchies, Laura B., Eli J. Finkel, James K. McNulty, and Madoka Kumashiro. "The Doormat Effect: When Forgiving Erodes Self-Respect and Self-Concept Clarity.*" Journal of Personality and Social Psychology* 98, no. 5 (2010): 734-49. doi:10.1037/a0017838.

McCullough, Michael E., Everett L. Worthington Jr., and Kenneth C. Rachal. "Interpersonal Forgiving in Close Relationships." *Journal of Personality of Social Psychology* 73, no. 2 (August 1997): 321–36. doi:10.1037/0022-3514.73.2.321.

_____. "Forgiveness As Human Strength: Theory, Measurement, And Links To Well-being." *Journal of Social and Clinical Psychology* 19, no. 1 (Spring 2000): 43-55. doi:10.1521/jscp.2000.19.1.43.

Nudelman, Gabriel, and Arie Nadler. "The effect of apology on forgiveness: Belief in a just world as a moderator." *Personality and Individual Differences* 116, (October 2017): 191-200. doi:10.1016/j.paid.2017.04.048.

Pedersen, Sven H., and Leif A. Stromwall. "Victim Blame, Sexism and Just-World Beliefs: A Cross-Cultural Comparison." *Psychiatry, Psychology & Law* 20, no. 6 (December 2013): 932–41. doi:10.1080/13218719.2013.770715.

Riek, Blake M. "Transgressions, Guilt, and Forgiveness: A Model of Seeking Forgiveness." *Journal of Psychology and Theology* 38, no. 4 (December 1, 2010): 246. https://search.ebscohost.com/login.aspx?direct=true&AuthType=ip&db=edo&AN=ejs44828084&scope=site.

Rizkalla, Laura, Eleanor H. Wertheim, and Lisa K. Hodgson. "The roles of emotion management and perspective taking in individuals' conflict management styles and disposition to forgive." *Journal of Research in Personality* 42, (2008): 1594-1601. doi:10.1016/j.jrp.2008.07.014.

Sandage, Steven J., and Ian Williamson. "Relational Spirituality and Dispositional Forgiveness: A Structural Equations Model." *Journal of Psychology and Theology* 38, no. 4 (December 1, 2010): 255. https://search.ebscohost.com/login.aspx?direct=true&AuthType=ip&db=edo&AN=ejs44828083&scope=site.

Schlessinger, Laura. *10 Stupid Things Women Do To Mess Up Their Lives.* New York: Quill, 2002.

Shapiro, Francine, and Louise Maxfield. "EMDR and Information Processing in Psychotherapy Treatment: Personal Development and Global Implications." In *Healing Trauma: Attachment, Mind, Body, and Brain*, edited by Marion F. Solomon and Daniel J. Siegel, 198-99. New York: W.W. Norton & Company, 2003.

Witvliet, Charlotte V.O., Everett L. Worthington, Lindsey M. Root, Amy F. Sato, Thomas E. Ludwig, and Julie J. Exline. "Retributive justice, restorative justice, and forgiveness: An experimental psychophysiology analysis." *Journal of Experimental Social Psychology* 44, no. 1 (2008): 10-25. doi:10.1016/j.jesp.2007.01.009.

_____., Thomas E. Ludwig, and David J. Bauer. "Please Forgive Me: Transgressors Emotions and Physiology During Imagery of Seeking Forgiveness and Victim Responses." *Journal of Psychology & Christianity* 21, no. 3 (Fall 2002): 219. https://search. ebscohost.com/login.aspx?direct=true&AuthType=ip&db=b-sh&AN=7901758&scope=site.

_____., Thomas E. Ludwig, and Kelly L. Vander Laan,. "Granting Forgiveness Or Harboring Grudges: Implications for Emotion, Physiology, and Health." *Psychological Science* 12, no. 2 (2001): 122. https://journals.sagepub.com.

Williston, Byron. "The Importance Of Self-forgiveness." *American Philosophical Quarterly* 49, no. 1 (January 2012): 67-80. https://www.jstor.org/stable/23212650.

Worthington, Everett L., Brandon J. Griffin, Loren L. Toussaint, Camilla W. Nonterah, Shawn O. Utsey, and Rachel C. Garthe. "Forgiveness as a Catalyst for Psychological, Physical, and Spiritual Resilience in Disasters and Crises." *Journal of Psychology and Theology* 44, no. 2 (June 1, 2016): 152. https://search.ebscohost.com/login. aspx?direct=true&AuthType=ip&db=edo&AN=ejs44838491&-scope=site.

Worthington Jr., Everett L. *Forgiving and Reconciling: Bridges to Wholeness and Hope.* Downers Grove, Ill: InterVarsity Press, 2003.

_____. "Helping people REACH forgiveness of others." *Bibliotheca sacra* 170, no. 679 (Jul - Sep 2013): 273-85. *ATLASerials, Religion Collection*, EBSCO*host*.

_____. "Self-condemnation and self-forgiveness." *Bibliotheca sacra* 170, no. 680 (Oct-Dec 2013): 387-99. *ATLASerials, Religion Collection*, EBSCO*host*.

Whatley, Mark A. "Victim Characteristics Influencing Attributions of Responsibility To Rape Victims: A Meta-analysis." *Aggression and Violent Behavior* 1, no.2 (1996): 81-95. doi:10.1016/13591789(95)00011-9

Yamaguchi, Ayano, Min-Sun Kim, Atsushi Oshio, and Satoshi Akutsu. "The role of anger regulation on perceived stress status and physical health." *Personality and Individual Differences* 116, (2017): 240-45. doi:10.1016/j.paid.2017.03.053.

I FORGIVE

www.ingramcontent.com/pod-product-compliance
Lightning Source LLC
Chambersburg PA
CBHW072139090426
42739CB00013B/3226